EYES WIDE OPEN

Also by Frederic Raphael

Novels
Obbligato
The Earlsdon Way
The Limits of Love
A Wild Surmise
The Graduate Wife
The Trouble With England
Lindmann
Darling
Orchestra and Beginners
Like Men Betrayed
Who Were You With Last Night?
April, June and November
Richard's Things
California Time
The Glittering Prizes
Heaven and Earth
After The War
The Hidden I
A Double Life
Old Scores
Coast to Coast

Screenplays
Two for the Road
Oxbridge Blues

Short Stories
Sleeps Six
Oxbridge Blues
Think of England
The Latin Lover
All His Sons

Biographies
Somerset Maugham
Byron

Translations
(with Kenneth McLeish)
The Poems of Catullus
The Plays of Aeschylus (2 vols)
Euripides: Medea, Bacchae,
    Hippolytus
Sophocles: Ajax

Essays
Cracks in the Ice
Of Gods and Men
The Necessity of Anti-Semitism
Karl Popper: Historicism and its
    Poverty

EYES WIDE OPEN

A Memoir of Stanley Kubrick and *Eyes Wide Shut*

Frederic Raphael

ORION

First published in 1999 by Orion Media
An imprint of Orion Books Ltd
Orion House, 5 Upper St Martin's Lane, London WC2H 9EA

A CIP catalogue record for this book is available from the British Library.

Typeset by Selwood Systems, Midsomer Norton
Printed and bound in Australia by
Griffin Press Pty Ltd, South Australia

EYES WIDE OPEN

During the spring and summer of 1994, the William Morris Agency, in London and on the Coast, kept receiving mysterious calls from Warner Brothers, asking whether I was available to work on 'something'. Each time I asked them to find out what the something was, my agents were told that Warners were not able to tell them. It seemed to be an empty, teasing enquiry.

One day, Steve Kenis rang from William Morris in London and asked me whether I liked *The Prisoner of Zenda*. Was this what all the mysterious phone calls had been about? No it wasn't, but did I? 'Doesn't everyone?' The inescapable myth of Rudolph Rassendyl and Black Michael and Rupert of Hentzau was the first thing I ever adapted for the stage, at the age of twelve. At the last moment, we were forbidden to produce it because of the danger of someone being run through during our realistic swordplay. Ruritania is something one never quite outgrows. 'Why do you ask?'

'We-ell, an American TV company called and, as the longest of long-shots, they want to know if you would ever con*sider* writing it as a four-part mini-series. They know you'll have to be paid. And I told them they would have to pay more than the number they first thought of. They'd already thought of that.'

I said, 'American TV. Nine producers, fifteen commercial breaks. Forget it.'

'Fred, they want this to be quality. Will you go to Paris and talk to them? Peter Pieter – p, i, e – flies in on Wednesday.'

'We're booked to go to Menorca for a few days.'

'They'll pay almost as much as a feature and – this is the good news – it's just one draft. After you've agreed the way to go. A day and a night in Paris and you're on your way. *Menorca*?'

INT. BEDROOM. HÔTEL RAPHAEL. AVENUE KLÉBER. PARIS. DAY.

F.R. is dressing down to go to lunch in a restaurant which he has never heard of at an address off the Avenue Montaigne.

> F.R.
> I hope I won't be long. I should be back
> around three-thirty. Will you be OK?

> SYLVIA
> Just remember. If you don't want to do
> it, don't do it. I'll be fine.

> F.R.
> *The Prisoner of Zenda* – corresponds to a
> childhood wish. Freud's definition of
> pleasure. It could be fun. Couldn't it?

> SYLVIA
> American TV? Could it? Don't do it
> because it's there, will you? Or just
> because you hate not to get a job. You
> can always get a job.

> F.R.
> Sure. But do I want to wait tables?

Under threat, F.R. thinks being American makes the situation more amusing, or less humiliating. He kisses his wife and goes out.

INT. 'STRESA'. A SHOWBIZ RESTAURANT. PARIS. DAY.

F.R. is sitting with PETER PIETER's sidekick, an American TV executive whom we will call ED. The tables are close together. The food is Italian. There seems to be more noise than nourishment. F.R. is hungry. He and ED have been sitting in their tight corner, with a diet of breadsticks, for half an hour.

> ED
>
> Peter's kind of a law unto himself.

They sit some more. A lot more. They sit another half-hour, chatting about the movies and then about ED's mercurial boss who can really make things happen, but cannot get to lunch on time.

> ED
>
> He's built this business up from a small
> operation to a multi-million-dollar
> company in five years. He does things
> his way.

> F.R.
>
> And so do you, I imagine.

> ED
>
> He's a man who hits the ground
> running.

> F.R.
>
> (Looks at watch)
> Is he running in our direction, do you
> suppose?

> ED
>
> He landed. He went to the hotel to
> wash up. He'll be here. You'll like him.

It sounds like an order. F.R. is still trying to like ED. He is trying to believe that he is right not to get up and leave.

ED's mobile shrills. He clicks it on and then he listens, and listens. F.R. notices Jean-Paul Belmondo who is so tanned, so artificially, that he looks like a *crème brûlée* with white hair. This is the man who starred in *À Bout de Souffle*, which is pretty well where F.R. is at this point.

> ED
>
> That was P.P. He got off the plane, just like I said. And guess what? He went to his suite and lay down for a few minutes. An hour and a half later, he just woke up. He'll be here in twenty minutes.

> F.R.
>
> If they close the kitchen, I just may dive out of the window and into the moat.

> ED
>
> Excuse me?

> F.R.
>
> Have you ever read *The Prisoner of Zenda*?

> ED
>
> I read some coverage. This is strictly P.P.'s baby. Why?

Most of the CUSTOMERS are already leaving as PETER PIETER comes into the restaurant. He looks as if he has eaten several meals already today. He is young and rumpled. He is less apologetic than aggrieved, and aggressive.

He slumps into a chair and scans the menu with one eye. With the other one he glares intimidatingly at the people he has kept waiting.

> P.P.
> I overslept.

> F.R.
> That sounds like an accusation. Do you have a suspect?

> ED
> Frederic has some truly wonderful ideas for the project.

> P.P.
> Let me tell you what I want to do.

F.R. looks through the window and can see the shining Belmondo using his now antiquated charm on a blonde who seems still to see him as he was in Godard's film. OVER THIS: PIETER tells F.R. an elaborate story about how he is getting money from a US network which *thinks* he wants to make a TV series whereas, in *fact*, he wants F.R. to make a movie script out of Anthony Hope's book so that, when negotiations break down with the Americans, 'we' can be left with a screenplay ready to be made into a major motion picture (oh for the days when there were minor ones!).

F.R. listens and listens. He affects to admire PIETER's acumen and to share his ambitions. Of *course*, PIETER goes on, and on, to say that he hopes to do many, many more projects with F.R. ED nods so much that he never manages to finish his *lasagne* with burnt, curled edges.

EXT. THE RESTAURANT. DAY.

> P.P.
> We're going to draw up the contract
> right away. I'm staying at the Ritz.
> Otherwise I'd give you a lift back to
> your hotel.

He gets into the grey limousine which has been waiting for him.

> F.R.
> I think I'll walk back to the Raphael.

> ED
> I'll walk with you. The sooner we start
> the bonding process, the better.

F.R. looks like a man who now understands the full meaning of the slogan above the entrance to Dante's Inferno.

INT. BEDROOM. HÔTEL RAPHAEL. DAY.

> SYLVIA
> You must've had a good lunch.

> F.R.
> Ah ... no. Why?

> SYLVIA
> Nearly four o'clock.

> F.R.
> Can happen when you start lunch at a
> quarter to three.

SYLVIA

Kenis called. He wants to talk to you
urgently.

F.R.

He urgently wants to hear that I've
agreed to do this shit. He's going to be
urgently disappointed.

SYLVIA

Disappoint him. *Please*.

F.R.

Think of those cracks in the tennis
court. What do we fill them with
except money?

The telephone rings.

KENIS

(On phone)
Fred? How did it go?

F.R.

Are we actually committed to this
thing?

KENIS

(As before)
In principle.

F.R.

The guy was an hour and a half late for
lunch. And he was hungry. Imagine
how late he's going to be when it comes
to paying me money.

                    KENIS
(As before)
OK, new business. How do you feel
about working with Stanley Kubrick?

                    F.R.
(Covers receiver, to SYLVIA)
Stanley Kubrick!
(To KENIS)
What's the project?

                    KENIS
(As before)
I don't know.

                    F.R.
Is it this thing I heard about set in the
23rd century? In another galaxy. I *hate*
other galaxies.

                    KENIS
(As before)
They want to know, are you available?
That's all I know.

                    F.R.
Yes, I am. *Aren't* I? Frankly, even if I'm
not, I am. I mean ... I'm not *contracted*
to *Zenda*, am I?

                    KENIS
(As before)
Morally maybe.

F.R.

Morally he was an hour and a half late.

KENIS

(As before)
No reason you can't do both things.

F.R.

True. I have two hands. But I don't have
two stomachs. I'm never going to keep
those people down.

KENIS

(As before)
Don't go away. Somebody's going to
call you. I have them on the other line.

F.R.

(As he puts the phone down)
Stanley Kubrick. Jesus Christ.

After a long few minutes, the telephone rang again. It was a
sidekick, asking if Stanley could call me the next day. I said that
we would be in Menorca by mid-afternoon and gave him the
number of the hotel. There was another pause and then the
aide came back to say, 'He'll call you either tomorrow evening
between six and eight or on Thursday at the same time.'

On the flight to Menorca, my mind flashed back to the
evening in 1972 when I had first (and last) met Stanley
Kubrick. Stanley Donen – who was living in London, in Montpelier Square – had asked us to dinner. Sylvia had to stay in
the country, looking after our third child.

Donen had been a legendary director ever since *On the Town* and *Singing in the Rain*. I first met him in 1964. He had just had a huge hit with *Charade*, starring Cary Grant and Audrey Hepburn. When I was asked to go to his office in Hamilton Place, I expected to meet an elderly egomaniac. I was greeted by a man not much older than myself who told me how *great* he thought *Nothing but the Best* was. 'They all say it's because of the director,' Stanley said, 'but I know it was the writer.' *Nothing but the Best* was the first screenplay of mine to be produced. Stanley Donen had already directed forty films. Would I consider working with him? Would I not?

INT. FURNISHED APARTMENT. VIA FRANCESCO FERRARA. ROME. NIGHT.

It is now the autumn of 1964, a year after F.R.'s first meeting with Stanley Donen. F.R. and SYLVIA have decided to take their children to Rome for a few months, during which F.R. has written a screenplay for Stanley Donen called *Two for the Road* in which, he hopes, Audrey Hepburn will star. F.R. has recently sent the completed first draft to S.D. and is waiting for his reaction.

Before working on *Two for the Road*, F.R. has written the script for *Darling*, which is now being directed by John Schlesinger at locations in Tuscany and in Capri.

It is, it seems, too late to hear anything tonight from Stanley Donen and F.R. is collecting the dozens of index cards on which the whole of *Two for the Road* has been set out, and edited, before being sent to London. F.R. sits there re-reading his own script, trying to believe that it's as good as it should be.

Then the telephone rings.

F.R.
(As if he didn't know, or hope, who was at the other end)
Pronto.

DONEN
Freddie? It's Stanley.

F.R.
Oh hello, Stanley.

DONEN
I just finished reading the script or I would've called you sooner. I nearly called you half-way through but I was afraid that might look silly. It's going to be way the best thing I ever had anything to do with.

F.R. sees before his eyes a montage of S.D.'s movies. It stars Astaire, Kelly, Coward, Hepburn, Sinatra, Peck, Loren, Taylor.

F.R.
(Who knows he shouldn't say such things, but always does)
You don't think it's possibly slightly too long?

DONEN
I love it. I want to do it just like it is.

Stanley never went back on his enthusiasm. Nor did he ever depress me with the doubts expressed by all the studios, except the last one he went to, Twentieth Century Fox. Only when he had good news did he share it with me. I never had a happier or more privileged time in the movies than during the making of *Two for the Road*. Stanley Donen told me that all he really cared about (though he certainly wanted a hit) was that I should feel that he had made the movie I had in my mind's eye when I wrote the script. Helpful people had warned me that he was a tyrant and a typical Hollywood producer–director and that I should watch my back. He was neither a tyrant nor typical. In good times and in bad, he is the best of friends.

The night I first met Stanley Kubrick, I drove up to London in the red Mercedes 280SL which Sylvia and I had bought only after seeing Audrey Hepburn and Albert Finney in *Two for the Road*. The other guests at Stanley Donen's house were the Kubricks (Christiane played the German girl who sang in the *bistro* at the end of *Paths of Glory*), Ken Adam (production designer on *Dr Strangelove* and *Barry Lyndon*) and his wife, and Lord Goodman.

For some reason (lack of easy conversation perhaps), we played a silly after-dinner game. Each of us was given a few matches and each in turn had then to say something (improbable) that he or she had never done. If anyone else *had* done it, he or she forfeited a match. Whoever had most matches at the end was the winner.

Stanley Donen said, 'I've never been in an underground train.' Most of us pitched in a match.

I said, 'I've never slept with a movie star.' Stanley Donen pitched in a match.

Lord Goodman (Harold Wilson's and who all else's lawyer) said, 'I've never taken legal advice.' We all pitched in matches.

What did Kubrick say? I *think* he said, 'I've never played games like this.'

I remember talking to him about *Spartacus*. For all its grandiose production values, it was one of the rare movies about the ancient world which a classicist could enjoy (Robert Rossen's *Alexander the Great* was another). I did not know what a miserable time Kubrick had had during *Spartacus* (it determined him never again to be a servant of the studio system, though it was a resolution he could never *entirely* honour). I singled out the scene where Crassus calls on the slaves to identify the man Spartacus and (supposedly) save their own lives by doing so. I told him how, the previous New Year's Eve, Sylvia and I had been on a train to Colchester with a man who had been in a prisoner of war camp in Germany. At some point, in 1942 or 1943, the SS had paraded all the English prisoners and ordered any Jews to take one step forward. One or two did so. The SS officer yelled out that if there were any others, they had better admit it by the time he had counted to three. The menace in his voice somehow alerted the prisoners to what might happen to the few Jews who were being singled out. One, two, at the shout of three, *all* the prisoners stepped forward. 'Pretty good scene,' Kubrick said.

I hoped that I had taken the opportunity to advertise my desire to make a movie about ancient Greece. I had been impressed by *Electra*, a recent novel by Henry Treece. The heroine of his retelling of the often retold myth was a village girl who imagined herself Electra. Having argued that one could do a movie about the myth without decking it with fluted columns or regal affectations, I later sent a copy of Treece's novel to Kubrick. He did not acknowledge it.

Sylvia and I landed and checked into the waterfront hotel which had been recommended as restful. Stanley did not call that evening. Sylvia and I spent a sleepless night, but not because we feared that he would not call: the hotel disco was directly beneath our room. The young of Menorca boogied till three. We did not sing along.

The next afternoon we slept. We went for a walk. We came back to the hotel at six-thirty.

'He's probably had second thoughts,' I said.

'He's been second-thinking for months,' Sylvia said.

'He won't call. Bet you. They're like that.'

'So who do you think that is on the telephone?'

'Probably the manager. Asking us to dance.'

F.R.: Hello.

S.K.: Is this Freddie? This is Stanley. How are you?

F.R.: Pretty good.

S.K.: Is this a good time?

F.R.: Absolutely.

S.K.: Good. So listen, are you free to work on something with me?

F.R.: I have something I sort of said I'd do, but for once I'm willing to dump it. If you really want me to do something. I have to tell you that I've seen every movie you've directed since *The Killing*. I never saw the earlier ones – *Killer's Kiss* and –

S.K.: *Fear and Desire*. You don't ever want to see those.

F.R.: So ... what's happening?

S.K.: Will you read something if I send it?

F.R.: Of course. What is it? A book?

S.K.: It's a piece of material. How do I get it to you?

F.R.: Is it, ah, science fiction?

S.K.: Who told you that?

F.R.: (Covers mouthpiece, to SYLVIA) *Christ!* It's science fiction.

S.K.: (Overlapping) Because no, it's not. It's something else.

F.R.: Fine. Listen, we're here for a few more days and then we're going to our place in France.

S.K.: I'll get it to you there.

F.R.: Stanley, forgive me, I have to get something straight. I'm not bullshitting here. I have this deal pretty well set with these other people. If I'm not going to honour it, I have to dump it like ... today. You're the only person I'd do this for. I have this conscience about those things. I also have this bank manager. (No laugh) So ... are you definitely offering me this movie or what?

S.K.: I don't know yet if it's something you're going to want to do.

F.R.: Can I be the one who decides that?

S.K.: You'll have to be.

F.R.: OK, so – forgive me – but if I want to do it, do you want me to?

S.K.: Sure.

F.R.: I have your word on that?

S.K.: You do. So ... where do I send the material?

(F.R. gives S.K. the directions and the conversation ends)

F.R.: (To SYLVIA) *Fear and Desire* is the picture of his I couldn't remember. Figures, doesn't it?

FedEx brought a package to our French house the day after we got there. It consisted of pages 203–296 xeroxed from a grey and dated-looking text. The author's name and the title had been cut out. As I hunched apprehensively over the wide pages, the antique air of the print reminded me of a novella which Fred Zinnemann had sent me in his old age. It had been set in the Alps, which he had always loved. I very much wanted to work with the director of *High Noon*, but I could not persuade myself that there was enough 'stuff' in the story. He went ahead with someone else and made a clinker. It was his last movie, but he did not regret its failure too much. 'I loved that last chance to work in the mountains,' he told me later, 'but you were quite right, of course, not to do it.'

The novella which Kubrick had sent me was set in Vienna at – I guessed from the absence of cars or taxicabs – the end of the last century, perhaps earlier. What was I to say if I could not see a movie in it? What did Kubrick want of me exactly?

The story concerned a doctor, Fridolin, and his wife, Albertina, who have been to a 'masquerade ball', where they were separately propositioned, returned to their apartment in an unusually amorous mood and passed a night of unusual passion. The next day something has changed between them and, after putting their little daughter to bed, they begin to analyse their feelings, and desires, of the previous night. As a result of his young wife's guileless confessions about her dreams and desires before she was married, and during their engagement, Fridolin – the doctor – begins to have ambivalent feelings about his wife. She tells him specifically about a young man with whom she would certainly have had sex, had he asked her, during a holiday in Denmark.

Albertina's apparently naïve honesty excites Fridolin to a comparable, perhaps slightly vindictive, confession. He tells of a 'quite young girl ... with loose blonde hair hanging over her shoulders and on one side over her delicate breast'. There is a meeting of eyes, and desires, between the girl and Fridolin, who 'sensed an emotion so intense, so far beyond anything that I ever experienced, that I was not far from fainting'. As with Albertina's blond man, there was no consummation, no further meeting: 'What I have told you happened on the last day of our stay in Denmark. Otherwise I don't know what might have taken place.'

After they have agreed (with ambiguous sincerity) in the future always to tell each other such things, Fridolin is called out to the bedside of a patient, a councillor, whom he finds dead when he arrives at his apartment. The councillor's daughter and devoted nurse is exhausted by her ordeal. Perhaps because her guard is down, the young woman suddenly confesses her love for Fridolin. Hardly has she done so than her fiancé arrives, together with some of the dead man's family. Fridolin is glad to escape, but he is in no hurry to go home. He walks the streets and, as if by chance, wanders into a street where a young prostitute approaches him. He goes with her to her room, but her youth and a certain squeamishness prevents him from making love to her. Still he does not want to go home. He goes to a third-rate coffee shop where a pianist is playing. Soon he recognizes a man sitting opposite him as a certain Nachtigall, a one-time fellow student with a 'soft Polish accent and a slightly Jewish twang'. Having dropped out of medical school, he became notorious for behaving in a rather reckless way (exciting an anti-Semitic remark, he recalls, from a Jewish banker in whose house he misconducted himself).

The two men have a drink and start to reminisce. Very soon Nachtigall begins to intrigue and then to excite Fridolin with what he is about to do. To make a living, Nachtigall plays the piano at certain rich houses, very late at night, during which what sound like very sophisticated orgies take place. So scandalous are the proceedings (and so beautiful and – perhaps – recognizable the women) that Nachtigall is blindfolded as he

17

plays. He can guess what happens, but it is, we gather, more than his life is worth actually to see anything. Fridolin wants to know how he can get in: do they have tickets, or what? They have only a password. Nachtigall says that he will be collected by a carriage and driven to an address he does not know. The guests at the orgy will all be in fancy dress and masks. Fridolin races to a nearby theatrical costumier where, by chance, he once paid a medical visit. He means to be back in time to learn the password from Nachtigall, whose reluctance to reveal it lacks conviction.

It is very late, but the costumier, a dodgy character called Gibiser, lives on the premises. Fridolin persuades him to rent him a monk's outfit and, as he does so, becomes aware of the presence of two men who appear to have sexual designs on the mentally retarded but sweetly breasted nymphet 'daughter' of Gibiser (she recalls the young girl who so thrilled Fridolin when he saw her by the seaside in Denmark).

Fridolin is both outraged and titillated by the retarded temptress. He warns G. about the consequences of pimping for underage girls. Then he runs off in his monk's cowl and mask in order to find Nachtigall again, who now – sure enough – tells him the password: 'Denmark'. Shortly afterwards, he hails a hansom and follows Nachtigall's carriage to its secret destination.

Fridolin is nervous as they approach a grand suburban house, but he is resolved to go through with his voyeuristic adventure. He walks up the drive and joins other masked revellers as they go inside. The password 'Denmark' seems sufficient to allay suspicion. He finds himself among a handsome and beautiful company who seem, somehow, to recognize each other's right to be there. A woman guest appears to intuit that he is an interloper and warns him to go away before it is too late. He prefers to brazen his way in.

He imagines that he has got away with his imposture, and ignores yet another, urgent, warning from the beautiful woman who, for some reason, feels concern for him. Suddenly, there is movement and all the women are naked. Conscious of his loneliness, he is accosted by a couple of menacing gentlemen who demand the password. Fridolin again offers 'Denmark', but they tell him that that is the password to gain entry and that there is another for inside the house. Fridolin affects to have forgotten it, but they are neither appeased nor amused.

Fridolin is taken into a side room where there are only men. He is threatened by a hostile crowd. One man seems to take command and orders him to remove his mask and declare who he is. Fridolin says that he will do so if the others will, but he is denied such satisfaction. He seems about to be seriously beaten up, perhaps killed, when the beautiful woman who earlier begged him to be gone comes into the room. Confronting the men alone, she offers – indeed demands – that Fridolin be spared and that she take his place as a scapegoat. Fridolin at first refuses:

' "Impose what punishment you wish, gentlemen, I won't let this woman pay for me."

' "You would be unable, in any case, to change her lot," the cavalier in black said very gently. "When a promise has been made here there is no turning back." '

Powerless to prevent the beautiful woman's sacrificial gesture, Fridolin is whisked out of the room and put into a carriage which moves off at speed.

The carriage goes so fast, so recklessly, that he wants to get out, but he cannot. Eventually, however, he is delivered to a point near his home and, confused and exhausted, returns to find his wife waking from a dream. Having hidden his monk's cowl in a closet, he lies down beside Albertina as she tells him the next erotic instalment of her dream-life. He is obsessed with the woman who, apparently, took his sins upon herself and wonders whether it was all a charade.

Albertina tells him about a long and disturbing dream from which she has just wakened. Guilelessly, she infuriates Fridolin with an elaborate narrative in which her Danish lover makes love to her in a scene of multiple love-making (which, to my mind, prefigured the one in Antonioni's *Zabriskie Point*).

As Albertina is enjoying shameless sex with her lover, she can somehow see her husband being arrested in a town far below her. He has been shopping for luxuries for her which she does not want. Even when he is scourged and seems on the point of crucifixion, Albertina remains, in her dream, more contemptuous than distressed.

This long account of his wife's insouciance, in the face of his degradation and imminent death, arms Fridolin with fresh indignation. His wife's dreamy infidelity seems to warrant his resolve to find the beautiful woman who volunteered to be punished or to die in his place.

Fridolin sleeps uneasily till early morning. Then, leaving his wife in voluptuous solitude, he goes first to the hospital where, to all appearances, he conducts his medical rounds with due diligence. As soon as possible, however, he goes to the seedy hotel where he knows Nachtigall to have been staying. The clerk tells him that the pianist has already left. Two men came for him and more or less forcibly persuaded him to accompany them to an undisclosed destination.

He returns his monk's cowl to the costumier. Gibiser has clearly paid no attention to his admonishments, since one of the paedophiles of the previous night is only just leaving the shop without shame or apology.

Fridolin rents a carriage and finds his way back to the house where the masked ball took place. No sooner has he driven up than a servant comes with a 'last warning' to back off and search no more.

Frustrated, he returns to the city, still determined to solve the mystery. More, he is now determined, by Albertina's confession of her own dream of infidelity, to take all the sexual opportunities which he previously spurned. However, when he visits the councillor's daughter, he finds her both unappetizing and unavailable; she is about to leave town with her fiancé and will never see Fridolin again. The young prostitute, to whom he brings a little care package of nourishing food, has been taken to hospital: she is either syphilitic or tubercular and will not be back for some time, according to another whore whose advances do not appeal to him.

Finally, Fridolin reads in the newspaper of the mysterious poisoning of a 'Countess' in a smart hotel to which she returned, late at night, escorted by two men. She has been removed to hospital unconscious. There is no evidence that it is the same woman, but Fridolin is now exhaustedly hyperactive. He jumps to the conclusion that coincidence is evidence. He hurries first to the hospital, where he is told that the woman has died. He then rushes to the morgue, where his medical qualifications gain access to the current corpses. Sure enough, the Countess is already among them. He inspects the body without being sure whether or not these are the remains of the beauty who offered to save him. The recently dead are already beyond recognition. Nevertheless, he is (so the text subtly indicates) *almost* sexually excited by the allure of the female body recumbent before him. He bends over her, 'as if magically allured'. He is called to order by the pathologist in charge of the morgue who asks, as Fridolin leaves, 'Was it she?' Fridolin hesitates and then nods 'without saying a word'.

Outside, he realizes that his adventure is over. He goes

home. On the pillow beside his sleeping wife, who is again in bed, he is horrified to find the mask which he hired from Gibiser (a Freudian error, it seems). He tells Albertina the whole story, as if it were the only way to salvage their marriage.

At the end she says, 'I think we ought to be grateful that we have come unharmed out of all our adventures, whether they were real or only a dream.'

'Are you quite sure of that?' he asks her.

'Just as sure as I am that the reality of one night, let alone that of a whole lifetime, is not the whole truth.'

'And no dream,' he then says, 'is entirely a dream.'

Dozing together, dreamlessly, husband and wife seem to be reconciled. They are wakened by a 'victorious ray of light' and by the 'clear laughter of a child' coming to greet them.

SYLVIA: What do you think?

F.R.: What do you?

SYLVIA: It's ... a little bit ... *dusty*, isn't it?

F.R.: But interesting. *And* a little bit dusty. I wonder who wrote it. Probably Schnitzler, possibly Stefan Zweig. It's very dated. And the translation's so ... stiff. Quite a bit of it's pretty silly and pretentious. Those overwritten dreams! But there's something ... convincing about it.

SYLVIA: I never did like dreams in movies.

F.R.: You know why they never work, don't you? Because the dreams that you dream don't have a *frame*, do they? Not like our vision, let alone like the frame of a picture or a movie.

SYLVIA: What're you going to say to him?

F.R.: Also ... dream space – whatever it is – it isn't equally, consistently ... *dense*: you notice details, close-ups, but there isn't an image that you can – what? – *scan*, is there? Not like what's been photographed or even seen through your eyes. You're *in* a dream, not its viewer, *aren't* you?

SYLVIA: Perhaps he knows what he wants to do about the dreams.

F.R.: Jesus. Can he *really* want to make a movie set in Vienna in 1890 or whenever it is? No cars, no telephones ... 18-something? It's so dated and yet it's ... strangely ... *something*, isn't it? Erotic? If nothing else. Is it anything else?

SYLVIA: He has to know why he wants to do it. Ask him.

As I waited for Kubrick to call, I went back over the text and marked the key elements. I could imagine a movie somewhat like Buñuel's *Belle de Jour* which calmly juxtaposed the plausible and the extravagant, the dated and the modern. Would Kubrick want to follow in famous steps? He must surely have some specific intentions. I did not know at the time that he had been trying to find a way of making a movie out of this particular novella for more than twenty years. One thing was certain: having been solicited to ride a famous tiger, I was resolved not to fall off, if I could help it.

S.K.: Freddie? This is Stanley. Did you have time to read it yet?

F.R.: Only twice.

S.K.: So, what do you think?

F.R.: Who's the author?

S.K.: Is there a movie there?

F.R.: Is it Arthur Schnitzler? I'm sure there's a movie. Depending on what movie you want to make. Or is it Stefan Zweig? It's one or the other, isn't it?

S.K.: Did you like the story?

F.R.: It's ... kinda maddening. It's good, but it's not *that* good, is it? Those dreams, do you want to have dreams in the movie?

S.K.: I don't know what I want exactly.

F.R.: For me, what's interesting about dreams in stories is what people *say* about them. How they describe them more than what they describe. I'm more interested in hearing about your dreams than in seeing the footage. *Aren't* I? We want to see and hear *her*, not what she says she sees. Have you ever seen a convincing dream sequence?

S.K.: I don't know. We can talk about that. We'll have to. Do you want to work on it or not?

F.R.: Of course I do. I was afraid it might be science fiction.

S.K.: Don't you like science fiction?

F.R.: I never read it. I never feel remotely interested in people who are going to be alive three centuries after I'm dead, do you?

S.K.: I don't know about people. Situations, yes.

F.R.: Are you still working on this A.I. [*Artificial Intelligence*] thing they say you are?

S.K.: Not right now.

F.R.: Also I don't know what kind of vocabularies people will have. It takes place in New York after the ice caps melt, is that right?

S.K.: Possibly.

F.R.: Venice on the East Coast. They won't talk like New Yorkers do now, will they?

S.K.: No? Why won't they?

F.R.: The sound of their voices'll be different without crowds in the streets. No subway, no cabs. They'll have a whole different set of expressions. Bound to.

S.K.: You may be right. What about our story? How do we do it?

F.R.: Are you thinking of doing it in period?

S.K.: Period? *No.* In New York. Today. In the present. I shoulda said. What do you think?

F.R.: I think, basically, thank God is what I think, about where and when. But ...

S.K.: Think you can do it?

F.R.: With a lot of work. This isn't just a case of ... adapting, is it? It involves, well, *translation.* Out of *fin de siècle* Vienna. It's Schnitzler, isn't it? Into modern New York.

S.K.: Think you can do it? Think it's dated?

F.R.: That's part of the ... challenge.

S.K.: Dated in what way?

F.R.: No cars, no phones, but that's not a problem.

S.K.: What's the problem?

F.R.: Underlying assumptions. Which are dated, aren't they? About marriage, husbands and wives, the nature of jealousy. Sex. Things have changed a lot between men and women since Schnitzler's time.

S.K.: Have they? I don't think they have.

F.R.: (After thought) Neither do I.

S.K.: OK, so who do I talk to about your deal? Do I talk to William Morris?

F.R.: Yeah, please. In California. Do you know Ron Mardigian?

S.K.: No. But I'll talk to him. How soon can you start work?

F.R.: How soon can we settle the contract?

S.K.: OK.

F.R.: It's not Stefan Zweig, is it?

S.K.: I'll get things started with Mardigian.

F.R.: Stanley...

S.K.: Yeah?

F.R.: Have I said how pleased I am to be doing this? I am. Very.

S.K.: William Morris, California, right?

The only other living director whose aura ever seemed as impressive to me as Kubrick's was Joe Losey. *The Servant* did not knock me out as *Paths of Glory* had, but (thanks in good part to Pinter's script) it was excellent. One day in 1964, when we were living in Rome, I had a letter from Losey asking me to work with him. Honoured, I went to see him in Wellington Square as soon as I got back to London. He received me *en maître*, reclining on a *chaise-longue*. The darling of *Cahiers du Cinéma* seemed dazzled by his own reputation. We discussed several ideas and parted with affectations of enthusiasm. Later, he asked me to adapt Roger Vailland's *La Truite*, a novel I thought without substance. He went ahead and made a movie which he later acknowledged that he wished he had not. He did not thank me for having been right.

Losey had decamped from California during the McCarthy witch-hunt, unlike the 'Hollywood Ten' who were indicted as 'unfriendly witnesses'. Billy Wilder said of them, 'Only two were talented, the rest were just unfriendly.' Kubrick told me that one of the most famous blacklisted writers, Dalton Trumbo, worked on *Spartacus*, which was based on the novel by Howard Fast. Stanley agreed with Wilder's view of Trumbo: he proved verbose and self-importantly protective about his script. Fast too had been a Communist, but there was no shit about him.

In the Sixties, when ranking producers agreed verbally with an agent on a deal, writers could be fairly confident that signature of the contract would happen in due course, though sometimes not until after shooting was over. By the Nineties, no such trust remained. Kubrick called Ron Mardigian and made a very swift deal at my 'usual' price. Screenwriters, like most talent in Hollywood, are quoted on an almost official stock-market. If you are seriously reluctant to do something, your price can rise until the offer becomes, the producer hopes, irresistible. If you are eager to work on an idea you love, and want to give it all you've got, you will get less for it than for work you wish you had never accepted. Kubrick did not haggle and Mardigian did not push him too hard. So far, so swift; then the lawyers came in. The studio would not release any money until documents had been signed and countersigned. I would not start writing, as opposed to *thinking*, before the first payment. The writer's money comes in slices, before and on delivery of the first draft, likewise the second, likewise the 'polish', and none of it is released until contracts have been, as *Variety* sometimes puts it, 'inked'. Somewhere on a far horizon is 'the back end', the payment which will be due if the movie is ever made and the writer has credit. While the lawyers kept each other busy, Stanley suggested that we meet and talk. 'Sooner the better,' I said.

On the day fixed for me to come out to his house, I took a couple of my books from the shelf to give to him. My purpose was less ingratiation than to remind him that Naboth had his own small vineyard. My new novel was called *A Double Life*. Perhaps the title would be taken as a warning that I was not merely a mechanic for hire.

Kubrick sent a local 'black' cab from St Albans (it was actually white). Once at St Albans, we left the honey-coloured cathedral to our right. It was mounted in surroundings of suburban banality, like a beautiful thought in a crass paragraph. Skirting the city, we drove along a country road and, after many twists, turned left through ornate green metal gates. They recalled Fridolin's visit to the country house where the orgy was to take place. We went past a Victorian Gothic lodge, down a private road rustily white-fenced from empty meadows, and skirted a small colony of gabled houses which were not quite mansions. Striped with damp sunlight, it was a scene of dignified autumnal melancholy. We forked left, past signs announcing PRIVATE PROPERTY, and over some sleeping policemen to another gate, which was closed. The driver got out to press the necessary buttons. He had to do it again sixty yards further on.

The house was huge, but not grand. It was a rather low, very wide, Victorian pile, with a pillared façade. There was an ample gravel courtyard and an air of pungent desolation. The place was heavily protected, but what riches were there to protect? It seemed more like a gargantuan cottage than a mansion. Across from the main building was a large brick stable block which appeared to contain offices. Several unpolished cars were parked on the gravel. The taxi stopped and I got out and went to the modest blue front door with a gable over it.

Kubrick opened the door. He was wearing a blue overall with black buttons. He might have been a minor employee of the French railways. He was a smallish, rounded man (no belt) with a beard which less defined than blurred his features. His black eyes were enlarged by big spectacles. He seemed shy as we shook hands. 'You got here.' He spoke as if unused to speech and not comfortable with company, even when he had invited it. I felt as if he had suffered some trauma which almost made him lose confidence in his person, though not in what he could do. He appeared both vain and self-effacing.

He led me through the huge house as if it were an abandoned factory or a bankrupt preparatory school, a place where people once milled about but which had then been evacuated. It was now more like a repository, full of disordered belongings, clean junk which might never be arranged in useful order.

INT. WORK ROOM. KUBRICK'S HOUSE. DAY.

It has a wooden roof and several tables laden with more clean junk. A published volume of Christiane's paintings is unshowily displayed, white-jacketed, in a stack of wide books. Her colourful landscapes and red and yellow floral pieces hang on most of the walls. The paintings have no shadows.

Large windows look on to a walled lawn which is wide and deep but not formal. Hell, is that a *peacock* out there?

A dog is asleep in a basket by the open door on to the lawn. No other houses are visible along the low horizon. A yew hedge to the right closes off the view.

F.R.
I brought you something of mine to
read.

29

S.K.

(Takes A Double Life*)*
I read this already.

F.R.

Damn: I signed it for you. Tell you
what: sell the copy you have.

S.K.

You read the story again?

F.R.

And again.

(Offers a slim volume)
This book you probably haven't seen.
Based on the myth of Gyges.

S.K.

OK. So what do you think: What're the
main problems?

We sat on upright chairs and talked. I knew that Stanley had
been a ranking chess player. It was as if I had been rung by a
cinematic Kasparov and there was now a board between us. It
was time to start measuring up, if I wanted to make a great
game of it. Even if I did, he was probably looking forward to
exhausting and humiliating me. For a quality game, both
players had to be at their best, but one had to be better and
would be the victor (chess is a game of bloodless sadism and
schemed execution). As the writer, I was sure to be saddled
with the black pieces; my best hope was to respond effectively
when under attack, as I expected to be. In terms of getting the
job, there was, I believed, nothing to fear (the numbers had
been fixed and contracts were being prepared), but I did not

want to begin our *mano-a-mano* by making a callow move.

Kubrick's manner remained mild, even modest. There was perhaps something deliberately intimidating in having brought me so far out of town, so clearly into his world and out of mine (in the Mediterranean, the man who displaces himself to visit another is conceding his superiority, by the very fact of travelling to see him, in no matter how swanky a conveyance). Never mind; the guy needed me or why would I be there?

Having left South Kensington an English novelist, I could believe that I had arrived in St Albans an American writer. I was born in Chicago and first went to school in New York. I like working in the movies not least because I feel rejuvenated by an American art form. What kind of work is it exactly? Film is at least as much a *sport* as an art. It demands concentration and stamina (so does sport) and it is in many ways playful: it calls for fancy footwork and quick responses. Solemn souls may regard lightheartedness as a kind of blasphemy, but solemnity is not always a characteristic of worthwhile work, nor irreverence of facetiousness. Even surgeons sometimes joke at the operating table; such chat need not affect the steadiness of their hands or the seriousness of their purpose.

I wanted to impress and delight Kubrick; he had, after all, chosen me (and taken his time doing it) and I wanted him to be right. I had no knowledge of his reputation as a colleague; books about celebrities, especially in the business, are either hatchet jobs or sponsored eulogies. Kubrick was a great filmmaker and I wanted to see this thing through, whatever it was. If I could never hold up the cup (he was already cast as the champion, should the movie ever be made), I could perhaps last until the final. I had to combine tact with forthrightness, deference with independence. The social nuances of screenwriting distinguish it from writing fiction. As the novelist Gabriel Fielding once said, 'Authorship is a rat-race in which you never get to meet the other rats.' In the movies, you meet them. Loyalty is not their most obvious quality. The screenwriter can be a kind of HAL, waiting without hope of reprieve for the captain to decide that he can fly on without him. All contracts these days tend to have 'cut-off' clauses, a point at which the writer can be paid off. My business (and my sport) was to make myself indispensable.

F.R.: For me the major ... not problem ... *weakness* is that it's a good story, but it's not a great one. Its final irony is a little too neat. You start with the parents with their little girl and you end with them and her. It's cute but it turns all that happens into a dark tale that gets tied up with a flourish like a pat little bow. There's no progression, is there?

S.K.: What else?

F.R.: Those dreams, that kind of stuff was fresh when Freud was. They don't read very convincingly to me. I wonder what Sigmund would have thought of them. Not a lot, I would guess. All that dialogue and such accuracy of recall, it's all so ... literary ... The author has to have read Freud, doesn't he?

S.K.: Freud and Arthur knew each other ... *Damn!*

Stanley banged the flat of his hand, hard, on the table. He was seriously vexed. How long did he hope to conceal the name of the author (who was now revealed indeed to be Schnitzler)? What point was there in hiding his identity from someone with whom a deal had already been made and who surely could be trusted not to ... do *what*? It was possible that the story was in the public domain, but why would I want to infuriate Kubrick by trying to steal a march on him? I suspect that his concealment of the source of the text had been little more than a game which he was playing with himself and against me: the warm-up. He did not remain piqued for very long. In fact, he looked at me through those large glasses as if I had achieved some petty victory during our opening moves. Strangely enough, after I had taken that first pawn, as it were, he became much more relaxed.

I expected strong views on precisely how he wanted the story transferred to New York, but evidently he hoped that this was a problem that I could handle. I was relieved; surely I should be better placed to please, and perhaps astonish, him if he had no precise expectations. The only idea which came out of our first conversation was that there should be an incident at the party at the beginning of the story which would require Fridolin – or whatever he came to be called – to display his medical skill on a female guest with whom his host (and patron) was having a clandestine erotic encounter upstairs, while his wife entertained the company below. I imagined the millionaire giving a showy Christmas binge in a mansion rather like the Frick Museum. When I made the mistake of saying that the latter was on 'Central Park East', Kubrick grinned and said, 'Central Park East is Fifth Avenue.' He collected my pawn with relish.

The mistake reminded me of when Sylvia and I had dinner, in the early Seventies, with Faye Dunaway and Marcello Mastroianni. I paraded my Italian, with courteous ostentation, but I was made nervous by so famous a companion. At one point I mentioned that I had been born in Chicago, but instead of saying '*nato*', I concocted '*nascito*, which made Mastroianni laugh quite a bit. Later, I asked him, in English, how it was that he never flinched from parts in which he played impudent cuckolds, sad homosexuals and the kinds of characters which Dirk Bogarde would have called 'weak'. *'Beh,'* Marcello said, *'cinema non è gran' cosa'*: cinema is no big deal. I could not imagine Stanley Kubrick saying the same. For him it was the *only* deal. (Mastroianni, who had been an architecture student when Visconti discovered him, said that he found greater pleasure in building houses than in acting.)

Stanley and I talked and talked and would have talked some more, had I not looked at my watch and seen that it was nearly half-past two.

He said, 'Do you want something to eat?'

'Beats having a migraine.'

'You suffer from migraine?'

'If I don't eat and I have to ... perform.'

'Let's go in here, see if there's anything we can eat.'

We walked from one long room into another. On a refectory table, next to stacks of books and boxes, there was a tureen of soup, cold breasts of chicken, salad with cubes of Gruyère cheese cut into it, lettuce and watercress with raspberry vinaigrette. There was fruit salad in a big bowl.

Stanley said, 'Feel like eating any of this?'

'Looks fine,' I said.

'Then let's eat it.'

It was as if there might be other rooms, with fancier meals in them, and I had settled for the first deal I was offered.

Stanley said, 'Do you like New Zealand wine?'

He was already opening a bottle. Again I was conscious of the delicate white hand that he had slapped on the table when he said 'Arthur.' As he strained at the cork, I remembered Billy Wilder doing the same thing and saying, 'Forty-five years of masturbation and I still don't have a muscle in my hand.' Stanley poured me a glass of white wine. 'Two twenty-five a bottle. What do you think?'

I sniffed and sipped. 'I think it tastes like two seventy-five.'

'OK,' he said. 'Help yourself to whatever you want. What's happening when he goes upstairs?'

'She's been having sex and she's OD'd on something and Fridolin – whatever we're going to call him.'

'He was Frederic in one version I had.'

'Truffaut always said that actors never really lose themselves in characters who have the same first names as they do. I'm the same. I only use Frederic ironically or Fred for comic relief. Fridolin takes care of her. Doesn't he?'

'What's your wife's name by the way?'

'Sylvia.'

'*Sylvia*? You don't mean that.'

'I don't call her that. But I do mean it. I call her Beetle. But that's another story.'

'In that same version, the wife was called Sylvia.'

'Whose version was this, when?'

'Call him anything you want to call him. Her too. Albertina's a little . . .'

'Proustian?'

'Fancy. Keep it simple. So what happens when he goes upstairs? Why can't they be having sex up there?'

'Don't we need to keep the real erotic fireworks for the *other* party? This one has to be superficially nice and elegant, amorous certainly, but not erotic.'

'Maybe we shouldn't have anything too much happen upstairs. Maybe it's enough that both of them have the experiences Arthur describes and that's it.'

'They can have those as well.'

'You like the idea of the girl upstairs.'

'I like it for what it can bring to the plot. It ought to lead to something.'

'Maybe.'

Kubrick was not indecisive; he was postponing decision,

which is by no means the same thing. Perhaps I was not alone in being nervous; he seemed reluctant to lay down a line which might inhibit invention. As soon as I made a comment, he backed away, as if he had taken his finger off the piece he seemed about to move. The chess player studies old games, but he cannot rely on them to supply winning moves, except against inferior players. He thinks, and then he thinks again. We ate and talked and then we just talked.

After a while, we went into what had evidently been the billiard room. There were still markers and cue-racks on the walls, but no table. Most of the floor was covered with news-papers with unfamiliar print. When Kubrick went to pee, I looked closely and saw that they came from Djakarta.

On his return, I asked him what particularly interested him about Indonesia. He looked puzzled. I indicated the news-papers. 'Oh,' he said, 'not a lot. I was only checking the size of the ads for *Full Metal Jacket*. Making sure they're as big as they should be according to the contract.'

I said, 'I wouldn't mind a pee myself.'

He led me along corridors and down steps and around corners and into the kind of facility you would expect to find in a club house. There were two separate cubicles side by side. As he went to leave, I said, 'How do I find my way back?'

'Stick to the left-hand wall,' he said. 'You'll get back finally.'

The house had been built for a South African millionaire before the Great War and he had, you felt, commissioned it by the cubic yard. It seemed nothing like a *home* whatever. It was a vast shell for the shrewd snail who found protection in it.

As it grew dark, I thought (without dread or enthusiasm) that Stanley might ask me to stay to dinner. I have a horror of protracted evenings in distant places when I do not have a car parked outside. Something about Stanley's house had the allure of Bluebeard's castle. One did not know, or care to guess, how many screenwriters had died and been buried in its recesses.

We had got no further in Schnitzler's story than the visit Fridolin pays to the flat of the dead councillor, during which the weary daughter declares her love for him, before Stanley looked at his watch.

S.K.: So, how do you feel?

F.R.: Fine. Tired, but . . .

S.K.: Did we do anything useful?

F.R.: I think so. I think maybe the girl passing out upstairs could work. I'm not sure. Can I . . . play around with it . . . see if I want to use it?

S.K.: Use it or don't use it. We don't want to spoil the orgy. That's going to be a problem when we get to it.

F.R.: It's the same problem that's going to come up a lot: the whole thing is like a dream. A lot of things almost happen in the story, but very little is actually spelt out or actually comes to anything. I think the whole thing is meant to be read as a dream, don't you?

S.K.: Whole thing? What do you mean?

F.R.: It's called the Dream novella, after all. And how come that when Fridolin gets to the so-called orgy – where nothing except naked women actually *happen* – the code-word is 'Denmark'? Bit of a coincidence, isn't it, when Albertina's dream man is also from Denmark. And so is the young girl that Fridolin sees on the beach.

S.K.: It can't *all* be a dream.

F.R.: Because that's not what Schnitzler meant or because it's not what you want?

S.K.: If there's no reality, there's no movie.

F.R.: Tell you what, let's not have it all a dream. But it still is in Schnitzler's book. Look at it again, if you don't believe me. He sees the whole Hapsburg world as a dream, don't you think?

S.K.: So how are we going to work?

F.R.: How do you want to? I'd really like to make a start, see what I can make of it. Unless you're careful, you can talk so much, you leave it in the dressing-room.

S.K.: Start how?

F.R.: Go away and do a chunk. I'd like to feel free to translate it the best way I can, bearing in mind what we've said, but ... see what I can come up with. I'll tell you if I hit any rocks.

S.K.: Are you happy to start right in working on your own?

F.R.: Yes. I don't have to *be* happy, but it's the only way I am. It's a story that deals with the unconscious. I may as well tap into my own, which I don't find easy to do in public.

S.K.: So when can you start?

F.R.: As soon as I've seen a contract.

S.K.: Can't you start right away?

F.R.: Stanley ... I'm very glad to be doing this, but you know that we all carry the scars of things that happened before. I'm ready to start *thinking* – I have started, as you can see – but ...

S.K.: OK, so ... if I tell you you can start, there'll be no problem with the contract ...

F.R.: I'll believe you. I *do* believe you.

S.K.: And you won't write anything.

F.R.: I'll think and we can always talk.

S.K.: On the telephone?

F.R.: I don't like leaving home any more than you do. I'll do it, but I don't like doing it. Work is when you have pages in the evening you didn't have in the morning.

S.K.: OK. Want me to call you a cab to take you home?

F.R.: It's too far to walk.

S.K.: Pages. Reminds me. I understand you want to ... go work by yourself. But ... you know what I'm going to ask you, don't you?

F.R.: Only too well.

S.K.: So, when you've done a chunk, thirty, forty pages, will you send them to me?

F.R.: You're the only director in the world I'd say this to, and I say with great reluctance ...

S.K.: Which I understand.

F.R.: Yes, I will.

S.K.: I just don't want you to go a long long way down some road I don't want to follow. It's a waste of your time and ...

F.R.: Pages. Jesus. I dread doing it and I'll do it. Not just because it turns screenwriting into something like Penelope's tapestry, forever being pulled to pieces just as it seems about to be finished.

S.K.: OK. Why?

F.R.: Also because I'm bound to leave some trailing wires that I either don't want to have to explain or, possibly, won't be able to – wires that I have a hunch will tie up with events in the later part, even though I haven't precisely worked them out yet. I hate a story that doesn't tie up, not neatly necessarily, in terms of plot, but in terms of overall shape. Don't you?

S.K.: Did you see *Full Metal Jacket* yet?

F.R.: I told you. I've seen everything except *Fear and Desire*.

S.K.: You know where the title came from? *Full Metal Jacket*?

F.R.: It's the name of a kind of bullet.

S.K.: Did that have an overall shape?

F.R.: Its overall shape was that it refused to have an overall shape. Wasn't that the point? You denied the viewer the smallest hope of second-guessing your intentions. No tragedy, no comedy. No tears, no laughter. Category-defying. Aristotle would've hated it.

S.K.: Maybe that was a mistake.

F.R.: But you don't think so?

S.K.: Thirty or forty pages, the first act, as they say, will you let me have that much?

F.R.: I said I would.

S.K.: But you won't start right away?

F.R.: The minute I see a contract. Until then . . .

S.K.: . . . you'll do some thinking. Me too. Taxi'll be here in five minutes. Where are you going to think? France?

27.10.94. Journal entry: 'He is, I begin to suspect, a movie director who happens to be a genius rather than a genius who happens to be a movie director. My difficulty with him will be to guess what he really wants of me. His may be the same. I shall probably find that, as usual with good directors, he wants only the competences which he cannot supply for himself. Once I have delivered them, they will seem so paltry to him that he will easily persuade himself that it was less that he did not possess them than that he was too busy to deploy them. I have been selected to be his outside caterer, but it will still undoubtedly be his party. We had an enjoyable afternoon, in the sense that the "bonding process" certainly began, but if he had not been a famous director, should I have been anything but vaguely intrigued by the lazy splendour of his manor and the strangely passive curiosity of the man?'

SYLVIA: So how was he?

F.R.: How was he? How was *I*? Sounds like a sexual question. And in a metaphorical way it is. Don't tell anybody, but from going to see Kubrick, a screenwriter can get a better impression of how it feels to be a woman than from reading *Fanny Hill*. You don't know exactly what he wants, but you know he wants he doesn't know what and hopes you can supply it. He has virtually no *ideas* at all. He's like Diaghilev with Cocteau: he wants to be surprised by joy. He was more like a producer than a director.

SYLVIA: Directing comes later probably. Nice?

F.R.: Polite. Almost tentative. Seven years since he made a

movie. He needs one. He probably has other things going on too, but ... he needs one.

SYLVIA: What kind of film does he want it to be?

F.R.: He didn't even *hint* in any specific way. He just wants it all transferred to New York in the present. I remember he once talked to Terry Southern about making a blue movie with name actors and great photography. I'll bet that's what's partly behind this, but he never talked about the sex, except that – maybe this is significant – at one moment he pointed out how movies always portray sudden passion and rushes of blood in the elevator, but they never deal with *married* sex, with the desire that suddenly replaces domesticity with almost violent ... You know. What he wants is the naked woman at the refrigerator door as she remembers to put the chicken away before she goes to bed.

SYLVIA: Interesting.

F.R.: Nice parents who read bedtime stories and then change into the strangers to each other that they need to be if ... There always has to be some unfinished business in a marriage, doesn't there? If it finishes ... there's nothing to be continued, except niceness, or resentment. That's the strength of the Schnitzler – it *is* Schnitzler by the way – he's smart enough (and on the nose enough!) to know about the sword in the bed. I told him I wasn't starting work, not work-work, until we got the contract.

SYLVIA: Do we have to stay in London?

We decided to wait for the contract at our house in the Périgord. Once upon a time, I was credulous enough to work for months without a contract, or payment. In the Sixties I believed that a certain producer and director were friends and that we were all partners in the project. After two years, I went on a brief holiday. My friends immediately hired someone else to do a 'polish' (which made everything she touched duller). Although none of the rewrite remained in the script that was later shot, I discovered that she had been well paid. When I reproached my partners, they smiled at my *naïveté*. It was time I learned about the way the business functioned. I will always write novels and stories and essays without prospect or thought of payment. I will never do as much for movie companies or their smiling touts.

Autumn in the Périgord is a time when the forests turn red and yellow, russet and brown. Truffles grow like goitres where knowing dogs can find them on the roots of oak trees. *Cèpes* bulge in the humid fields. Fattening walnuts split their green husks and hang perilously until the late October rains bring them down in clattering generosity. I wrote some stories and made anxious marginal notes on the Schnitzler, so that I could persuade myself that I already knew, roughly, what I was going to do when the contract was signed.

When Kubrick called, he asked if I liked Kieslowski. I said that I had seen only *Three Colours: Blue*, which I found interesting but a little forced. How about the *Dekalog*? I had never heard of it. He immediately sent me the two fat cassettes which contained the set of films, about the Ten Commandments, which Kieslowski had made for Polish TV. As Sylvia and I watched them, I wondered what lesson I was supposed to learn from the tight sprawl of such uncompromising stories. Did Stanley want to make the Schnitzler as loosely framed and verbose as the *Dekalog*? The only thing which Kieslowski seemed to have in common with Kubrick was an obsession with the unpleasant. The episode about the murder of a taxi driver and then about the hanging of his murderer was as unblinkingly nasty as anything in *A Clockwork Orange*. Its lack of elegance made it almost unendurable. The only weakness in the piece was the glib observation by the odious killer that things might have been different if he had stayed in his village. Directors often fall for natty narrative 'twists'; their reading is rarely as sophisticated as their vision.

S.K.: This is Stanley Kubrick. Freddie there?

SYLVIA: (Calls) *Fred!*

F.R.: Hi, Stanley.

(Long and close friendship with Stanley Donen gives him the illusion that he already has a similar intimacy with S.K.)

S.K.: So what do you think of the Kieslowski?

F.R.: Amazing.

S.K.: I'll tell you what's amazing, he did all ten of those things in one year. Did you hear anything on the contract yet?

F.R.: I hear everything's going smoothly.

S.K.: Have you started yet?

F.R.: I've started thinking. A lot.

S.K.: So you haven't. Ten movies in one year, can you imagine?

F.R.: Sure. Do you want to do something like that? Because I'm sure you could.

S.K.: Think so?

F.R.: I'll write them for you, if you like. On one condition.

S.K.: What's that?

F.R.: I don't get paid till you shoot them, and that you shoot them.

S.K.: Sounds like two conditions to me.

F.R.: All we have to do is go to the BBC and tell them you want to do them.

S.K.: He had this lawyer friend of his told him the stories.

F.R.: There's no problem with stories. I'll write you some while I'm waiting for the contract.

S.K.: I'm going to call them soon as I hang up. You know, I've been looking at some pictures of Arthur. You look quite a lot like him, you know that?

F.R.: You want the movie to be anything like Kieslowski?

S.K.: I don't know. I think we have to take him into account.

F.R.: There's a lot of talk. You want a lot of talk?

S.K.: I can't say what I want. I want to do Arthur's story, but in New York, now. That's all I can tell you. I wish I could tell you more. I can't.

I went to my desk and, for the hell of it, began to write what I thought of as stories for Kubrick. Ingratiation and defiance were among my mixed motives. What fun to demonstrate what I could do when I was under no obligation to please or even to perform! Hoping to surprise and shock him, I planned a pair of stories set in the New York which I had not lived in for more than half a century. It is an almost voluptuous exercise to escape from English social nuances to the broad brutalities and smart talk of a city I sometimes think I should have stayed in. I started in the usual short story writer's prose, but as the stories thickened, I first intruded cinematic narration (in the style of a 'treatment', which always uses the historical present) and then switched for key scenes into the notation of scriptwriting. The stories gathered such pace and made such a claim on my attention that I began to dread the interruption of the completed contract. I bet myself that I could compile all ten of my decalogue before beginning with Arthur. I could then amaze Kubrick with what I could do for him without his even knowing.

7.11.94. Journal entry: 'I have had three more long and exhausting telephone conversations with S.K. To begin with, I was as deferential and thin-voiced as any hireling. I have become less inhibited. Cinematically, I have no doubt that he is a master. However, I have little fear that he is intellectually beyond my reach; I am not even sure how bright he is. Why is he *so* guarded? Laughter is loss of control; he substitutes grumbly little noises for it. He listens to my spiel with a kind of responsive taciturnity. He expects me to react promptly to him, but he takes his time with me. If he has begun to loosen up a little, the signs of it are in his freer use of anecdote – especially about Kirk Douglas – in order to lighten up our long, long conversations.

'He is at once disdainful of Kirk (whose name can be extracted from Kubrick, leaving only "cub" behind) and in awe, in particular, of his sexual competence and voracity. He told me that, on the set of *Spartacus*, K. – while waiting for his call – would survey the women on the studio tours which came round regularly. When he saw an attractive woman, he would send someone to talk to her. Given an opportunity to meet the star, who refused? When Kirk was called unexpectedly (as he always arranged to be) to go to make-up, he would regret that duty called, take a pace to go, then turn back and ask the lady if she would care to come to his trailer and have a cup of tea while he endured the tedium of the powder puff. How many of them had Kirk instead of tea, who was to say?

'It may be that Kubrick turned Kirk into the emblematic instance of the insufferable producer not only because he had been tyrannical but also because he had, at times, been right. According to some of Kubrick's biographers, there was a moment, before they started shooting *Paths of Glory*, when Douglas was more uncompromising than his young director (Stanley was not quite thirty at the time). On being handed a late rewrite of the script, Kirk was alarmed, and outraged, to find that Stanley had decided that the three doomed soldiers – selected at random for execution on trumped-up charges of cowardice – should be reprieved at the last minute. Kirk is said to have protested at this craven concession to box-office considerations. The original pitiless ending was restored and, thanks (perhaps) to Kirk, *Paths of Glory* became the uncompromising masterpiece we all admire. If Kubrick did indeed flinch from the tragic and appalling version which now seems to bear his hallmark, I suspect that it was less from squeamishness than from fear of financial failure. The one thing common to all of his movies is fascination with violent death.

'Whether or not Kirk stiffened Stanley's resolve, there was no doubt that Kubrick alone created the choking atmosphere of battle, as he did the disgusting dignity of the château where heartless generals (Adolphe Menjou and George Macready) schemed for promotion among elegant silver and Sèvres china. Before *Paths of Glory*, who had ever seen air-quality photographed? The motes in the château's sunbeams gave a depth to the screen which not even Welles had equalled. The clean air of headquarters declared itself too good for other ranks. Unadulterated oxygen seemed to have been siphoned off – château-bottled, as it were – for the brass. If the montage in *Paths of Glory* owed something to Eisenstein's *Battleship Potemkin*, the film had no message of or for humanity. It neither called for the overthrow of the ruling class nor did it advocate the brotherhood of man, in the facile style of Jean Renoir's *La Grande Illusion*.'

While still waiting for the agents and lawyers to finalize the contract, I finished the two long stories which I have since revised and are part of my recently published volume *All His Sons*. They owe nothing to Kubrick except that I had him in mind when I was writing them. If there is a harshness in them which is more natural to S.K. than to me, I shall not be giving him credit.

9.11.94. Journal entry: 'He has worked with a few actors more than once – Kirk, Sellers, Hayden, Rossiter, Quigley – but never, I believe with an actress. He has no favourite female star and there are few, if any, memorable women's moments in his movies. He remarked the other day that he and I were born too early (to enjoy the sexual opportunities of our juniors). But Kirk is older than we are. Stanley didn't challenge my remark that some people (like Fridolin) are born with a membrane between them and the reality which seems so enviably accessible to others. Being "behind the camera" is the objective correlative of that feeling, and perhaps its furtive cure: those who cannot live desire power over the living.'

The screenwriter never has the power a director has. Sometimes, however, he can have the illusion of it. Actors, and actresses, are often charmingly deferential in their approach, which can lead the writer to believe that he is more authoritative than he is. Diane Keaton once told me how much she loved a screenplay I had written. She had only one regret:

couldn't I have written her character with bigger tits?

Audrey Hepburn had had serious doubts when Stanley Donen first approached her with the idea of *Two for the Road*. Once she read the finished script, she asked Stanley Donen and me to come and see her at her house in Bergenstock. Her doubts had vanished; she became unquestioningly loyal to the project.

Familiarity doesn't always breed contempt (who could despise Audrey?) but it does breed familiarity, and a certain presumptuousness. Once we were shooting the movie, I was tempted to treat Audrey as one more actress whose business it was to speak the lines I thought right for her. There was a scene at the end of the film which they were soon to shoot and which, on the usual nervous re-reading, I decided was 'illogical'. I revised it and handed it to Stanley for distribution to Audrey and Albert.

When I next saw Audrey, I said, 'Did you get the new scene?'

'Yes, I did.'

'Much better, don't you think?'

'Freddie,' she said, 'have I so far uttered one word of criticism of one line of the script?'

'Not that I remember,' I said. 'Why?'

EXT. SOUTH OF FRANCE LOCATION. DAY.

AUDREY
I really do prefer the old scene.

F.R.
Audrey, believe me, you're wrong. The
old scene was messy and ... it made
no logical sense, if you look at it
carefully.

> AUDREY
> And the new one does.

> F.R.
> Which is why...

> AUDREY
> ...I don't like it.

C.U.: AUDREY smiles her best smile.

> AUDREY
> It's *so* logical. Would you mind reading
> them both with me? And then
> deciding?

> F.R.
> No. But ... really...

INT. AUDREY'S CARAVAN. DAY.

AUDREY and F.R. sitting on the narrow bed.

> AUDREY
> Which'll we do first?

> F.R.
> The old one, I think, because then
> you'll see...

> AUDREY
> *(Points to script page)*
> Start here, shall we?

> F.R.
> Fine.

(Clears throat, plays the lead)
'How long is this going to go on?'

AUDREY
(Pauses, smiles brightly)
'For ever...'

F.R.
(Puts down the script)
OK, you're right. We'll use the old
scene.

A kiss on the cheek can feel good too.

11.11.94. Journal entry: 'We have already spoken for more than ten hours on the telephone. I observe that I am becoming more aggressive, even mocking, when I disagree with him. But I am not deceived: no man is a hero to his valet, but no valet is for that reason a hero. S.K. senses reluctances and doubts with a kind of impatient sensitivity; he is too smart to discount my hesitations to agree with him and too self-contained to welcome them. He has decided that Schnitzler's dated and very European story can, and will, be translated to the US now and he resists any questions about its "relevance". (Why do I play the producer and raise such vulgar issues?) He has – in words he would never use – bought the "myth". It is only by seeing it in that light that I can get rid of its dust. But then, like a man stirring in his sleep, S.K. *almost* faces the mundane American reality which says that a couple like F. and A. would "get a divorce". Yet he has become enough of a European for the marital myth to have leeched on to him. (We are probably the two most long-serving husbands in the movies.) He cannot quite see that any durable myth is pretty well autonomous, and its plot, however elasticated, largely determined: Oedipus and Jocasta will never be able to avert trouble by spending more quality-time with their kids. What I dread and cannot help probing is the possibility that the Kubrick myth will perish under close inspection. I need him to be great, and yet I probe for his flaws. Like the nth wife, I cannot be happy until I have found the key and gone into that locked room in Bluebeard's castle and made myself unhappy.'

When the contract arrived, I sat down to read it at the kitchen table. An early clause stipulated that during the whole period when I was being paid I was forbidden to write anything else whatsoever. Since doing the occasional book review or essay is one of the ways in which I stay sane (because independent) while working on a movie, I was not about to make promises of that kind. Worse followed: a later clause declared that, in matters of credit, the decision of Stanley Kubrick should be final concerning who had written what line and who had had what idea.

I said to Sylvia, 'Sorry, but I can't do this movie.'

F.R.: (*À la française*) 'allo.

S.K.: Freddie? *Ici* Kubrick. Can you talk?

F.R.: Sure.

S.K.: Are you OK?

F.R.: In places.

S.K.: What's the problem?

F.R.: I just got the contract. Did you see the clause which stipulates that, in any case of disagreement, Stanley Kubrick shall be the sole judge of who wrote what line and who thought of what idea and that the writer promises to abide by that decision? I'm sorry, but I can't work under those conditions. I want to do the movie, I don't want to be a paid slave. And I won't be.

S.K.: Where'd you find that clause?

F.R.: Right where you had them put it, didn't I?

S.K.: What's the problem exactly? Why would I want to say I wrote something I didn't write? Why did I ask you to work with me on this? It's just a quick way to –

F.R.: Stanley, do you know the fable of the frog and the scorpion?

S.K.: The frog and the scorpion. Do I?

F.R.: There was this river and the scorpion wanted to get across.

S.K.: Oh yeah.

F.R.: So he begged the frog to give him a ride. And the frog said, 'You're a scorpion. If I give you a ride across the stream you know what you'll do: as soon as you're almost there you'll sting me and I'll die.' And the scorpion said, 'I won't. This time, I swear to you, I won't. I just need your help.' So the frog gives him a ride and as soon as they're nearly across the scorpion stings him, and as he's dying the frog says, 'What did you do that for? You promised.' And the scorpion says, 'I know I did. And I wanted to keep my word. But I'm a scorpion.'

S.K.: What's your point?

F.R.: You haven't heard the showbiz version. The director, who can't swim, asks the writer to help him cross the stream. And the writer says, 'When we get to the other side, you'll dump me and claim all the credit.' And the director says, 'I know that can happen with directors, but you can trust me. I just need to get to the other side.' So they cross the stream and the director dumps the writer and claims all the credit. That's one version. *My* version is, the writer says OK and the director gets on top of him and half-way across the stream the writer dumps him into the water and as he's drowning, the director says, 'What did you want to do that for? I promised you I'd be straight with you.' And the writer says, 'I know, but I happen to have read the first draft.'

S.K.: We don't have the clause, how do we settle credit?

F.R.: There's a thing called the Writers' Guild. I pay them a fortune and they do nothing for me except that they have this adjudication service. Just like they do in the States.

S.K.: OK if that's what you want. About the script, I've been doing some thinking.

F.R.: There's something else, Stanley. The contract says that I am forbidden to do any writing of any kind during the duration of my screenwriting period. That suggests that even when I've sent you pages and I'm waiting to hear from you, if it's technically in the period, I can't even write a book review.

S.K.: Why do you do those?

F.R.: Sylvia asks the same question. And the answer is vanity, and it gives me something new to get my mind around.

S.K.: That's what I want to avoid.

F.R.: Stanley, I may never do one, even while I'm twiddling my thumbs, but I won't be told I can't.

S.K.: It's standard.

F.R.: And I'm in breach if I write a short newspaper article? Or a ... Look, I won't give you short measure, OK? I promise you that. And that's all I'll promise. I won't work on another *script* for Christ's sake, but ... I won't be a slave. Servant maybe, slave no.

S.K.: OK. Now can we talk?

F.R.: Let's talk.

I was in a London cab one day when the driver told me that he had an idea for a script. I smiled and mentioned that everybody did. I was a writer myself. 'What kind of things do you write?' 'Oh, all kinds. Novels. Stories. Travel stuff. Movies. TV. Criticism.' He looked at me in the mirror. 'Know what? Drop the criticism.'

11.11.94. Journal entry: 'We talked, but what did we achieve? Well, we lubricated the lines of communication. What does he want this movie to be? Is it that he can't say or that he won't? Why *this* movie? He won't even say that. He can do anything he wants and he wants to do this, but he cannot say how or why, just *that*! Perhaps it is a puzzle that he has to solve, like a chess master who recognizes that the answer *has* to be a queen sacrifice, but cannot yet see how or why.

'He seems a little more human – commercial – than I might have hoped of a very great director indeed. He likes stars because they know what they are doing *and* because they fill theatres. My problem with him is that he is resolutely apprehensive of disclosing himself, even if it would serve his own ends. ("Show my hand" is what he should have said he never did, that night at Stanley Donen's.) I must have no expectations of gratitude or of genuine collaboration. I must make satisfied (or *fairly* satisfied) curiosity my best reward, apart from money, which seems at last to be on the way. I do not know and cannot quite guess what precisely made me attractive to S.K. What use does he hope to make of me? He doesn't want to be told what film to make, as A. or B. would. I am stage one of his rocket and I will, no doubt, fall away (or be ejected) when he has attained lift-off. Remember that. There remains *something* he wants, and is happy to have Warner Brothers pay for, but either he cannot or he dare not specify what it is. 'Is it typical of all success that it leads to fear and isolation? (Or is that true only of *Jewish* success?) Is there something peculiarly unsatisfactory about succeeding as a director, especially for someone who wants to be taken for intelligent? S.K. has been coshed by his own fame. He is, if anyone is, a *thinking* director; hence, perhaps, his dread of the "conceptual": he has no interest in *purpose* and refrains from declaring any big idea. He is so afraid of pretentiousness (and perhaps so attracted by it) that he refuses to say, maybe even to himself, why we are doing this story. He wants to strike out into undiscovered territory, but also to be sure that it contains the gold he needs to find there. He surrounds his palace with a security system that seeks to make the accidental as remote as a man can arrange. Yet the essence of all guardedness is that it awaits its intruder. In the myth, Bluebeard *wants* to see his wife go into the room to which he has forbidden her entry. That is what he married her for. S.K. is as nervous of the unexpected, the disconcerting, as he is keenly in search of it; one cannot give him what he expects, because that is not what he wants.'

In one of our long, long talks, I pointed out to Stanley how thoroughly Schnitzler's story was impregnated with Jew-ishness. The students who bump into Fridolin as he walks the streets insult and alarm him (and are, in fact, based on anti-Semitic fraternities of the period). He both despises them and fears that he has funked their insolent challenge. Nachtigall is a 'typical' Jew, a wanderer available for hire, outrageous but willing to be blindfolded and made a servant. The episode at the orgy in which Fridolin is literally unmasked, and called on to say who he is, seems to emphasize his alienation from the 'gentlemen' who manhandle him. Fridolin is an outsider, like every middle-European Jew, and his medical dignity, whatever untouchable status it may seem to bestow, somehow compromises his virility. Transferring the story to New York seemed to me to offer an opportunity for keeping the Jewish aspect of the story, however it might be modernized. Kubrick was firmly opposed to this; he wanted Fridolin to be a Harrison Fordish *goy* and forbade any reference to Jews. Perhaps this would keep the theme buried (and hence more subtle), but his main motive, I am sure, was the wish not to annoy the audience. He wanted to escape into myth and inhabit an alien character who, nevertheless, would be close to him. In the end, Fridolin was to be given the surname Harford, which – with Freudian neatness – does not sound very different from Hertford(shire), the county in which Stanley lived. It was not all that far from Har(rison) Ford either.

We discussed making the wife (who has no job or calling in the story) a painter, in order that she should not seem dated and parasitic. Of course, Christiane is a painter, which may help him to feel close to (or distant from) the character of

Albertina. Kubrick told me that Christiane's uncle directed *Jew Süss* for Goebbels. When Stanley met him, he said that he could, in fact, have refused the commission (or at least declined it), but did not. The most memorable sequence in the film is the last, in which Süss is hauled up, with a noose around his neck, in a metal case (something like the one still to be seen in the 'papal' castle at Peñiscola in Castellón in Spain). After a long sadistic dangle, the Duke nods, with a sort of merciful contempt, and the Jew is dismissed from life. It reminds me of what directors like to do to writers.

12.11.94. Journal entry: 'I suspect that Bluebeard likes his own wife to be "busy" at home; am I very different? It exempts a man from the need to be with her, but keeps her within the castle, a free prisoner. (Why is it important to men that their wives be *good at something else*? Better some*thing* else than some*one* else perhaps.) Is S.K. drawn to this improbable *donnée* by an inner compulsion whose origins – Freud, thou shouldst be living ... – he cannot surface? If so, the closer I get to what intrigues him, the more strenuously will he deny that I am getting there.

'He says that he does not want jokes (as if he has heard something disreputable about my cooking and is saying, "No garlic, OK?"). He said recently, "I don't want the kind of thing Stanley Donen might have made with Cary Grant and Audrey Hepburn." (Nice one, Kubrick.) This was in response to my suggestion of "You and Me" as a title. I need a title, and wish we had one that wasn't "*Rhapsody*", which is what Schnitzler's translator proposes. S.K. told me that he admired David Mamet's *House of Games*. Was he hinting that I should adopt Mamet's anorexic allusiveness? That kind of mannered dialogue and elaborate plotting determine and limit performance. Would S.K. welcome such constriction if I supplied it? Fat chance.

'What is most elusive about excellent directors is what specifically they are excellent *at*. In the case of the second- or third-rate it is easy to say: they are good at getting films to direct. In S.K., there is no sign of conceit except in the intensity of his anxieties and the wariness with which he greets *every* idea I offer. (Cf. My old producer friend Jo Janni in restaurants, after reading through a two-volume menu, "Have you got anything else?") S.K.'s aversion from wit spares me the most professional of all obligations – being funny is no joke – but beyond eroticism, what does he want of me? Our subject is desire. He refuses to be concerned with the mechanics of copulation – what Nabokov called "the porno-grapple" – but he seems to want to photograph feelings, to catch the impalpable and palp *that*. I think back to the sunbeams in the château in *Paths of Glory*; he dreams of capturing the *air* in Schnitzler's world and breathing it, furtively, into our New Yorkers.

'He seems to want to settle all kinds of things – where the dreams go, if not where they are, and *what* they are about, assuming as I tend to argue, that the present ones are too ostentatiously Freudian. I remember, but do not mention to Kubrick, the story about Louis Malle, when he had just made *Black Moon* at a budget of two million dollars. Billy Wilder asked him what it was about. Louis said, "Well, Billy, it's sort of . . . a dream within a dream." Wilder said, "You've just lost two million dollars." And so they had.

'At a certain level S.K. is keener that I should *have done* a script than that it should be brilliant or original. (*He* has to be the original one.) He does not care for me to surprise him; surprises are likely to stun and numb him (because they challenge his desire for complete control). He has hired me for reasons he cannot declare. If I am to reach the dangerous

ground which alone excites *me* in this voyage, I must treat
him as a false guide; I cannot ignore that he is at least as
much my enemy as my companion. He does not know our
destination any more than I do, but he must seem to do so,
in order to remain our leader. Directors are a cannibal breed.
Their nature is to seek out those whose destruction will give
them the greatest charge (and the squarest meal).'

The writer may believe, with whatever degree of justice or
modesty, that he has been responsible for the substance of a
movie. If it had not been for his lonely work, before actors or
technicians have been hired, nothing would have happened.
If he is the prime mover (Aristotle's term for God), he soon
loses his primacy. The production – the film-making – takes
place after he has completed most of his work. In the jostle
of egos as filming begins, the less that is said about the script
the better it probably is. The old saw is that movies are not
written, they are *re*written. However, if emendations and add-
itions patched together on the floor, or in urgent offices, may –
may – save the ship, they more often accelerate its foundering.
Tootsie is the exception which does nothing to disprove the
rule. Its apparently seamless unity derives from the last-
minute work of over a dozen writers, working one after
another. Shared screenplay credit gives the illusion of collaboration, but Larry Gelbart insists that he did not meet his
alleged co-author on *Tootsie*, Murray Schisgal, until they went
up together to receive their Oscars. I am not sure how eager
he was ever to meet him again.

Longing to deserve the accolade of *auteur*ship, directors
often seek to append their names to the writing credits. Their
habit is to be empowered to embellish scripts which they
were powerless to begin. The writer may be crucial to the
conception of a movie; he is seldom integral to the business

of shooting it. He has to take his chances with what powerful directors or demanding stars will do when he is out of the way. Studio contracts make sure that nothing can guarantee him against being dumped or rewritten, misconstrued or ignored. Directors are often unpunished serial-killers who appropriate credit from writers whom they have jettisoned or, so they judge, improved. As his Oscar acceptance speech showed, Stanley Donen is the rare instance of a legendary director whose pleasure it is to give credit to others.

14.11.94. Journal entry: 'I have the whore's consolations: whatever I am, he *chose* me; he chose *me*; *he* chose me. How many reasons is that to be happy? Is it my film or my literary work that led him to call me? There is something in me which I do not disclose, and perhaps he recognizes that, in me and in himself. We were both born in America and have lived for decades in England, albeit for quite different motives. We each have a certain New York buried in our psyches. Where we differ is that he lives in England without England really knowing it; and without knowing England. He is the most famous incognito since Bismarck was elevated to the rank of an unknown prince. A man goes round London pretending to be Stanley and hardly needs to pretend, since no one knows what the real Stanley looks like. His supposed double gets tickets to shows and gains entry to clubs merely by using his name. Something like the hero of Nabokov's *Despair*, this man has usurped another's identity without, so they say, looking in the least like him.'

(Added note, March 1999: 'The word is that the man who adopted Stanley's identity died a fortnight before S.K. There must be a myth about a man who knows that he is doomed to die because he no longer has a shadow.')

14.11.1994. Notebook entry: 'S.K. has come as near as he can to being a present absentee; he may challenge England with his work, but never with his person. He makes as little noise as possible; you might say that he was hiding not only from life but also from the angel of death, who will get no hints from him on finding the way to Stanley's address. A man who hides resolutely from death is obliged to mimic death itself; to lie that low is to imitate the dead.

'I'm tempted (too often?) to argue that any Jew involved in the arts is concealing – even as he displays – the sense of alienation which came of the Holocaust. Civilization's most moral citizen is the hypocrite; its best art is camouflage.'

S.K. was startled, and a little excited, to find that he had access, on his new computer programme, to a catalogue of world-wide sexual services, their price and the percentage likelihood of being mugged while on the way to enjoy them. The list began with the simplest item on the menu: One-Shot Cunt Fuck.

S.K.: I think we're about set, aren't we?

F.R.: Time to play ball.

S.K.: I saw something of yours on TV the other night. *Man in the Brooks Brothers Shirt.*

F.R.: Did they show that again?

S.K.: Pretty good dialogue. You wrote it, right?

F.R.: Miss McCarthy is almost as prosy as Arthur. I . . .

S.K.: And you also directed it?

F.R.: I made it a condition for doing the script and David Brown went along with it.

S.K.: He's a pretty good guy.

F.R.: I think so.

S.K.: He was at Warner Brothers one time.

F.R.: Briefly. I did a script for him there ...

S.K.: He came over with Ted Ashley and those people to a screening of *Clockwork Orange*. They all sat in the theatre and watched it and when the lights went up, nobody said a word. Ted Ashley didn't say a word. Neither did anybody else.

F.R.: Of course.

S.K.: Those people, that's what they're like. Some silence, OK? And then David Brown came up to me and he held out his hand and he said, 'Congratulations. It's a masterpiece.' Right after that, they all said the same thing. I never forgot that. He's a good man. He produced your movie?

F.R.: That's why he's a good man.

S.K.: OK, do you have a script of that? I'd like to have a script of that.

F.R.: I don't know. Why don't you call him? He does. He'd like to hear from you.

David Brown is one of the few people in the movies who calls you when you are *not* hot. If he asks a favour, it is usually to do something which you would enjoy. On one of our trips to LA during the late Eighties, Sylvia and I were invited to dinner with David Brown and Stanley Donen at Valentino's (still the best Italian restaurant in LA). David was about to produce a series of short films for HBO (he scarcely needed the money, but he loved the work). He would really appreciate it, he said, if I would adapt Mary McCarthy's *The Man in the Brooks Brothers Shirt*.

'There's no money, but you might enjoy it and it'll only take you twenty minutes.'

'Who's going to direct it?'

'We'll find somebody good.'

'How about if *I* direct it?' I said. 'I'll write it for nothing if you let me do that.'

'Saves looking for anybody else,' David said.

God bless America, where decisions are (or were) taken without prolonged delays. I wrote and, a year later, directed *The Man in the Brooks Brothers Shirt*. The single week of our shoot coincided with the hurricane which struck England and uprooted several ancient trees in our Essex garden. I scarcely noticed even when it nearly ripped the roof off the Shepperton sound stage where John Graysmark had built the trans-American railroad car in which Elizabeth McGovern and Beau Bridges were consummating an adulterous affair. Orson Welles called directing 'the ultimate train-set'; I had more fun than I ever had with my Hornby double-0. Cyril Connolly might have coined his phrase 'Narcissus with his pool before him' expressly to describe the bliss of cinematic command.

My first assistant was Derek Cracknel. On the first day, we were in the middle of shooting a scene during a huge storm when some incidental noise became audible. Derek immediately shouted 'cut'. He was, I dare say, right to avoid wasting time, but I sensed a crisis of authority. In principle, no one on the set says 'cut' except the director. Mark Rydell told me once how, on *The Cowboys*, 'Duke' Wayne had taken it upon himself to yell 'cut' when a stampede started going in the wrong direction. Mark knew he had to face Wayne down, and did; he had no more trouble. *Rite de passage*, am I right?

I said, 'Derek, I'm sure you had a good reason, but you do know – don't you? – that the only thing I really do on this set is say "action" and "cut". I don't want to hear anyone else saying my lines again, if that's all right with you.'

When I told Stanley Kubrick this story, he said, 'You got away with talking to him like that?' One day, on Stanley's set (during the making, I believe, of *The Shining*) Derek was making a longer fuss than usual about some delaying detail and Stanley finally said, 'Derek, piss off, willya?'

Derek pissed *right* off.

At the end of the day, Stanley said, 'Where's Derek? Something the matter?'

One of the unit said, 'Well, sir, you told him to piss off. And he has. For good.'

Stanley said, 'Surely he knows all I meant was fuck off.'

S.K.: Freddie, you know something? You should direct something else.

F.R.: Stanley, *Brooks Brothers Shirt* was a one-week shoot and they held my hand a lot. Plus, I happened to have David Lean's cameraman.

S.K.: So what? You're a pretty damn good director.

F.R.: Believe me, there isn't anyone I'd sooner have say that.

S.K.: You are. And that's why you're never coming on my set.

F.R.: I don't think I'm meant to be a director.

S.K.: Why not?

F.R.: Probably because it's too much like hard work. Not the directing necessarily, but getting to direct. And then when you do, if you do ... it all ... maybe it's better being a writer. For me.

S.K.: You don't think directors are artists, that what you're saying?

F.R.: I don't know. And it doesn't matter.

S.K.: You mean it does, and we're not.

F.R.: I just know that before even you can be the kind of artist you are (and Vladimir Nabokov said you were), you need actors and sets and lights and cameramen and tons of money and all kinds of stuff and all I need to be an artist, if I am one, is a pencil and a piece of paper.

S.K.: You sure know how to hurt a guy.

F.R.: Depend on it.

S.K.: So. Time to go to work, right?

15.11.94. Journal entry: 'Irwin Shaw, when rich and soused, still went to work as a writer every day. When someone asked him why he bothered to write novels, he said, "What else can you do in the morning?" I am lucky never to have been rich enough to be tempted to stop, even for a drink.'

November 1994. 'Time to go to work'; easily said, less easily done. I was an experienced writer in his early sixties, used – if not addicted – to the regular accumulation of newly written pages. At my age, Balzac had been dead for eight years; Byron for almost thirty. I was still nervous. I am nervous whenever I begin *anything*. Hemingway used to sharpen all his pencils before starting work in the morning and then he read through what he had done so far on whatever he was doing. I do the same; I am like a carpenter who runs his hand over a sanded surface and has to smoothe anything that snags. The important thing is to go ahead and create *something* which can then be smoothed. Ideas, however good, are not tangible. As Henry James used to say, '*À l'œuvre, mon bon.*'

I decided to christen Fridolin 'Bill'. He had to be called something ordinary and along came Bill. Albertina could be Alice. Once alone with that first blank page, the important thing is to fill it, fast. It is more than likely that it will eventually be cut, or modified. To try to get it right before you know what follows is a neurotic danger which replaces invention with anxiety. The best thing is to take a deep breath and, as Ed said of Peter Pieter, hit the ground running. *Cinema non è gran' cosa*? Any motto will do that gets you over those first hurdles.

I tried to imagine a film that Kubrick would want to make. I had played the willing scribe (as *The Hollywood Reporter* terms every screenwriter), but I was also a secret Pharisee: I hoped to show Kubrick that I was better than other men whom he might have recruited. I also wanted to induce him to make a movie I should like him to make. Only furtively could I intrude anything of myself, or even of my visual ideas, into his work, but unless I supplied something which no one else could, what point was there in playing the Sisyphus part? Sisyphus is the screenwriter's mythological patron saint. For resisting the Gods (the directors of the ancient world), he was sentenced forever to roll a huge rock uphill. As soon as he reached the top, his rock rolled back down to the bottom again (they always want another draft, you might say). Albert Camus said of him, 'We have to imagine Sisyphus *happy*.' Kubrick knew the story well enough to misquote it to me during one of our later conversations.

We had not discussed what kind of man our New York doctor would be, except that he should not be (manifestly) Jewish. I gave him the name Scheuer in order to convince myself of his reality. I had a friend called Jimmy Scheuer when I was at Ethical Culture, my first school, on Central Park West. The Scheuers kindly lent me and Sylvia their apartment when we first went to New York together in 1963. I appropriated it gratefully, and greedily, for Bill and Alice's residence.

I began, as usual, with the credits sequence. It is an area in which, more than any other, the writer can warm up without undue anxiety, since whatever he proposes can, and often is, jettisoned. It serves almost as a kind of 'leader', the name given to the length of empty film which enables the spool to be engaged in the projector.

I suggested that, with the screen black, we hear the voice of a young medical student as he whispers to himself the Latin names for parts of the female anatomy. He is revising for an examination in which he will need to know them. As the black lightens, we then find ourselves in an apartment on Central Park West.

We could start in the late 1960s or early 1970s, when Bill Scheuer is still a medical student. On the wall above the desk where he sits in his father's den is a framed reproduction of Rembrandt's *The Anatomy Lesson of Dr Nicolaes Tulp*. Bill could be looking at pages of detailed illustrations and drawings of the human anatomy, especially female. In the oppressive atmosphere of his parents' apartment, the dutiful, driven student is trying to match his father's expectations and achievements, of which framed citations on the walls offer calligraphic proof.

I imagined, intercut with evidence of the young man's serious attention to medicine, glimpses of the kind of erotic display to be found in the porno peep-shows which were to be found in arcades around 42nd Street during the 1960s (ah research, how invaluable it can turn out to have been!). One of these erotic images – of a dark woman wearing only garter-belt and suspenders caressing herself – is particularly delicious, as well as arousing, in its slow, almost balletic display of the female body. The woman looks at 'us' and invites desire and complicity.

This (remembered?) display is abruptly aborted by Bill's father, William Scheuer Sr, a respected professor and surgeon, who looks in at his son. Bill quickly turns another 'proper' page in his textbook, as if to conceal the image of the mas-turbating woman.

The clinical illustration (not erotic at *all*) clearly comes from a book – written by Dr William Scheuer – in an academic series in which there is a tell-tale gap on the shelves lining the den. We can sense the double bind of Bill's dutiful clinical studies with a frustrated longing for erotic experience.

I warmed to this projected opening. Isn't an element of self-excitement necessary to the conception of all but the prosiest fiction? What I wrote was meant to make me believe in Bill's 'reality' and also to stimulate me into living his life. We happened to have Arthur Schnitzler's *My Early Life in Vienna* on our shelves. I noted how he had been laid on his father's desk when he was first born and with what ambivalence he regarded the famous specialist (Schnitzler senior was a laryngologist) who inspired both his medical career and his rebellion from *bourgeois* propriety. I added to my credit sequence the suggestion that it be expanded to include glimpses of Bill's student life, including the dissection of his first cadaver (something of which the mature Schnitzler spoke with a shiver of candour) and the difficulty he could have had in remaining 'cool', as a student of anatomy, while seeking hotter pleasures as a young man.

After the first section, I advanced the action by twenty or so years (please, without putting up a 'card' to say as much). I replaced the Rembrandt *Anatomy Lesson* with a portrait of the late Dr Scheuer whose practice had now been taken over, like his apartment, by his son. We were to discover that the portrait had been painted by Alice, Bill's painter wife.

We had now reached the evening of the party where the husband and wife were to be amorously solicited by different people and from which they would return to make love to each other with unusual passion. It was, I thought, good to avoid the narrative weakness which led Schnitzler almost immediately to flash back from the beginning of his novella to what preceded it (it is tempting, but nearly always a mistake, to start with a striking moment and then to explain it retrospectively).

The credit sequence gave me an opportunity to display a number of my own ideas in a free zone, so to speak. They could provide evidence of my fertility, and any or all of them could be accepted or rejected. It was like giving attractive wrapping to a parcel before you quite knew what it was to contain. I was pleased by what, to my mind, established the kind of 'split' man that Bill was. I told myself that Stanley would be seduced into believing that I knew what I was doing. The sequence goosed me into the same conviction. I went ahead speedily (dialogue never goes well if it goes slowly). Sanding and polishing could, and would, follow. I did not want to send S.K. anything I could not, as they say, defend.

In fact, nothing of what I have set out so far turned out to appeal to Kubrick. However, it enabled me to gather pace. I had a similar experience when I took my Cambridge scholarship. The first paper was Latin Prose, my favourite subject.

I thought I wrote one hell of a Ciceronian passage and was so buoyed up by the belief that I had made a great start that I did the following papers in confident style. Three weeks later, I was, as they used to say, 'elected' to a major scholarship. When my tutor wrote to congratulate me, he advised me to read more Cicero and Tacitus; my Latin Prose paper had been 'disappointing'.

Perhaps part of my hold, such as it was, on Stanley was that he knew, and probably exaggerated, my academic credentials. He told me, during one of our warm-up conversations, that he never went to college. However, as a cub photographer for *Look* magazine, he found time to sit in on classes at Columbia given by Moses Hadas, Gilbert Highet, Lionel Trilling and Mark van Doren, whose son Charles agreed to cheat on a quiz-show (in this he was as much a pioneer as a scoundrel, since all such things are now likely to be rigged, like awards and – if you have the right buddies – reviews). Stanley had pressed his nose to the windows of the academy as Fridolin/Bill did/does to the world of unbridled sensuality. S.K.'s interest in the ancient world in particular was a tribute to teachers he never quite had. Prey to an inquisitive restlessness which was both endearing and demanding, he had an outsider's love of inside information. He relished, and indulged, the licence which fame gave him to call anyone anywhere and expect answers. He liked people to be smart, in the American sense, and he had a (Jewish?) respect for scholars. However, he could become impatient with the very experts on whom he had depended: Arthur C. Clarke, for instance, had become too regularly effusive in dispensing intelligence.

S.K.: He keeps sending me all these faxes. Pretty well every day I get a shit-load of stuff from him. Did you ever see the movie they made called *2010*?

F.R.: I did as a matter of fact.

S.K.: What did you think?

F.R.: I didn't stay till the end. It ... wasn't directed by Stanley Kubrick, was it?

S.K.: Know what they did? They explained everything. They told you what everything meant. Killed it. You tell people what things mean, they don't mean anything any more.

F.R.: You certainly didn't do that.

S.K.: Caesar's *Gallic Wars*. What do you think? Have you read it?

F.R.: Stanley, I read it in Latin when I was nine years old. I lie. I may have been ten. Possibly eleven by the end.

S.K.: OK, so what do you think?

F.R.: Pretty good book. Monty's memoirs before their time.

S.K.: Is there a movie in it?

F.R.: Caesar's *Gallic Wars*? Eisenstein thought there was a movie in *Das Kapital*. Pretty expensive. Especially building that bridge over the Rhine. And if you try to follow Caesar's recipe, there are some problems with what he meant exactly.

S.K.: Remember that scene between Caesar and the German guy ... after he's finally surrendered?

F.R.: Vercingetorix.

S.K.: Probably. Remember that?

F.R.: When he asks Caesar why he had to come in and ruin all their lives basically?

S.K.: That's a pretty good scene in there. Pretty good dialogue. We wouldn't have to change a thing. That's one hell of a scene, so all we'd have to do is kinda ... do it up to that point and then ... get to the end. Pretty amazing character, wasn't he, Julius?

F.R.: All that plain-speaking military man narrative concealing all those devious, completely egotistical motives and intentions. He was quite a bastard, old J.C.

S.K.: Wasn't everybody? Was he any worse than anyone else?

F.R.: Better and worse. The mark of the genius maybe.

S.K.: Think so?

F.R.: Not necessarily. Caesar had no reason to invade Gaul, except that he had an overdraft and that was the only way to repay it. The Romans didn't want Gaul, but he needed a power base and the war supplied it. He probably went too far or not far enough. If he'd conquered Germany, it might have been part of western civilization.

S.K.: That's a pretty good scene out there in the snow, I'll tell you that. What's the best book about him?

F.R.: Rex Warner did a couple of novels, in the Robert Graves style, which aren't bad. There's Mommsen, which is dated and very *Führerprinzip*ish, and Michael Grant did a very competent one. There's a new German one, which I have for review as a matter of fact ...

S.K.: What do you mean?

F.R.: I mean someone sent it to me for review. It's very turgid and a little too Mommsenish for my taste. I can send it to you. But it keeps telling us Caesar's motives and psychology.

The reason film could be the best medium for depicting the ancient world is that you can't film motive, can you? You can show how people behave and never get into why.

S.K.: How's the script coming? When are you going to send me something?

I reckoned I had four weeks in which to accumulate a suitable chunk to send to Kubrick before I was interrupted by Christmas festivities, and by the labours of love and shopping which preceded them. If I thought that I was making good progress (even permitting myself a measure of levity in the dialogue, although I avoided jokes), I had more than the usual apprehensions. Directors rarely offer early praise, for fear that the writer's foot will come off the accelerator. Kubrick was less likely than any other to break out premature champagne.

The fun of first drafts is concentrated in the opening sequences. The story has to command interest, but – in the case of the Schnitzler (God, I did wish it had a credible title!) – I was free, not to say required, to create a convincing modern, New York atmosphere. Nothing in the text was of the smallest help, which at least avoided inhibiting piety. I was particularly pleased with a scene, after a night of passionate sex, in which Bill becomes the doctor again and – before going to see the dead 'councillor' and his suddenly amorous daughter – gives a plump lawyer called Harry a check-up at the hospital. They talk generally about life and death and then, as a last precaution, Bill proposes to check his patient's prostate. He goes to put on a rubber glove to conduct the examination. His patient, Harry, lowers his pants and, out of our sight, arranges himself on the daybed in order to allow the doctor to do the necessary probe with his sheathed little finger.

Lying on his side, still with his legal glasses on, and his shirt and tie, of course, Harry looks philosophical. As Bill does his stuff, Harry talks about the way two guys can talk about life and death and the meaning of life and then one of them puts his finger up the other one's ass. Such was the dignity of man.

It seemed to me a very Kubrickish moment of accurate irreverence. Would it seem so to him? Would he be amused, or would he think only that I was making jokes? I thought no more about him than I could help. I watched the imaginary screen and listened to the dialogue. To my relief, I began to believe that Fridolin and Albertina had successfully crossed the Atlantic and could be naturalized without their accents being too obvious. It seemed that I could still work the old trick whereby, as a schoolboy, I had transposed the eighteenth-century letters of Junius into Ciceronian prose. *Mutatis mutandis* was the slogan to keep in mind; change only what needs changing, but then change it without piety or trace.

Although I had protested at Kubrick's attempt to hedge me contractually against all activity outside the Schnitzler, I was so thoroughly engrossed that it was a shock when John Schlesinger rang to say that he had now read a short screenplay of mine which was scheduled for a series, rather like the one which David Brown had produced, for cable TV in the States. I had especially asked that it be offered to John, who had seemed pleased. Now, however, he had some 'points', none of which, I thought, was very piercing. The main burden of his lament was that he was being asked to shoot my story in Canada only because John Boorman had been given so large a tranche of the budget to make *his* little film in France. Personally I should have been happy to shoot the film in Toronto. I asked John how he was and what was happening. A number of projects were, he assured me, likely to get in the way of his doing this one. He did not ask me what else I was doing.

S.K.: Freddie? Can you talk?

F.R.: Sure.

S.K.: So how's it going?

F.R.: Fine. I think.

S.K.: See the *Spectator* this week?

F.R.: I see nothing except the script.

S.K.: Well you should see it. It has this article, it's about the most anti-Semitic thing I've seen recently. Some guy called Cash who says Hollywood is a Jewish racket.

F.R.: Lucky Darryl Zanuck never found out. The guy probably only does it because it teases, and gets him into the paper. The *Spectator* kinda specializes in that stuff. I write for it myself sometimes. Not at the moment. Not at the moment.

S.K.: You ought to read it. This is nasty stuff, believe me. I'll send it to you. You have a fax?

F.R.: Yes, but I have to switch it over and it's a drag. I can imagine the article.

S.K.: I'll put it in the mail. You're going to need to have a fax, or how are we going to communicate?

F.R.: It works fine. I just have to run up and down stairs a lot.

S.K.: Why don't you have it downstairs?

F.R.: It's a long story. Do you want one?

S.K.: Make it as long as you want to make it. I don't think we should even think how long it is until a lot further down the track. Give me everything you've got, OK? Freddie?

F.R.: I will.

S.K.: I don't like scripts that just give you dialogue and stage directions, stage directions and dialogue. I need to know more about the whole ... what's going on. I even want to know what people smell like, you know? Anything you can think of that ... might be relevant. Or irrelevant, but ... know what I mean? You're a novelist. Make it like a novel, not like a Hollywood script.

F.R.: If that's what you want. But it may get pretty long. They don't like that.

S.K.: Who's they? There is no they. Not until there is. There's me and there's you and that's it.

F.R.: Best thing I heard since you said to cut that credits clause out of the contract.

S.K.: You're reviewing some book?

F.R.: I have to get to sleep somehow.

S.K.: So how long before you send me some pages?

At the bottom of my forty-second page, I had reached the point where Bill goes to see the dead man whose daughter is in love with him. I gave them a panelled apartment on the Upper East Side, rather like that in which we once spent an evening with a pretty publisher and his much older mistress. I made Schnitzler's 'councillor' into a senator and broke off before the scene in which Bill is embarrassed by the daughter's demanding confession. It would make a sweet downhill point at which to start again after Christmas.

F.R.: What do you think?

SYLVIA: It's good.

F.R.: Poor Belle! Who'd be a writer's wife?

SYLVIA: It's fine. You've brought them to life. What more can you do? I think he's very lucky.

F.R.: Is there *anything* you think . . . ?

SYLVIA: Maybe the opening is a little . . . elaborate.

F.R.: Maybe. But I want to make him . . . think. I want to engage the bastard, you know? If he doesn't like any of it, what does he want? I have to coax him out of his passivity. If that means *seeming* to have more directorial ideas than he does, well . . .

SYLVIA: Send it to him.

F.R.: I want to take one more look. I'll take one more look.

SYLVIA: Send it to him. What can happen?

F.R.: What can happen is he hates it, he wants me to start over, and over, and over. Remember Sisyphus? I do.

7.12.94.

Dear Stanley,

So: here are forty-two pages which take us to the point we agreed. I have made it as dense, and at the same time as generous, as I know how. In the eventual scheme, I suspect these forty-two pages will come down to something more like twenty-five, but I promised you a full version, and here is it.

I hope (and dare to believe) that the 'translation' has worked, without reading as if it were anything but an original text. It's for you to decide. I particularly like what I've done with the woman upstairs at the party and, as you will see, it fits seamlessly with the rest of the elements.

I have some ideas, more or less outlandish, about where the second half of the story can take us, and I think you may see that I have allowed for certain symmetries, which may or may not appeal.

As you can guess, it is like producing a quarter or a fifth of a baby: the feelings of nausea and effort are the same, but the embryo doesn't offer one the reward of even crawling yet. I do think there is life here, however, and I wait, with confidence and trepidation, for your verdict.

We are driving to our house in Essex and will stay there till Monday next. If you recall, we planned to see each other on Wednesday. I have kept it free, but should be glad if you would confirm when and where we should see each other.

Thanks for the *Spectator* piece. Of course the thing is anti-Semitic in the sense that there would be no point in writing it if either the author or the readership did not find it somehow *sinister* that Jews should have common interests (albeit often in cutting each other's throats) and if it was not assumed that Jews acting together must have some exclusive ambitions or vulgar purposes or both. On the other hand, it is typical, I think, of the pointlessness of modern malice, which is its own justification, that it need have no *intentions*, either political or metaphysical or even social. Hostility is what the English are now good at, though they lack the will or the means to get seriously excited over anything whatsoever. The last vestige of imperial vanity is angry impotence at those who can still do something. What Gentiles now want is that we should apologize to them. I have long and short answers to that one.

When we arrived at The Wick, our house on the Essex/Suffolk

border, where we always spent Christmas, I could only wonder what Kubrick was thinking. I re-read my pages and my letter. Had I said too much, or too little? Too much. As I waited for S.K., I read a novel called *Cloud on Sand* which I should never have started if Marty Scorsese (who proposed to produce the movie) had not recommended it to John Schlesinger. Imagining S.K. taking callous aim at me, I was reminded of the second duel scene in *Barry Lyndon* in which Barry (one cannot think of him without hearing Michael Hordern's voice on the commentary) has stoically to await the shot which will cost him his leg.

The suspense was so keen that we almost forgot about it. Sylvia was making mince pies. The house was full of wrapping paper and rooms in which one or other of the family was forbidden to go. My mother was coming for Christmas, so were Sarah and her children, as well as our sons Paul and Stephen. We had for years depended on the help of Jack and Isabel Smith, who cared for the house while we were away from it. Jack, who combined the offices of gardener and security guard with the unquestioning devotion to duty of a CSM in a good regiment, had been taken to hospital with a haemorrhage. Isabel was with him all the time. The prognosis was bad. I was slightly ashamed that I was reminded of a novel by Elsa Morante (once the wife of Alberto Moravia) in which the lives of an entire family are shattered and changed by the death of the loyal servant on whom their tranquillity depends. La Morante's novel was infinitely better than *Cloud on Sand*, on which I was due to pass screenwriter's judgement (in the last resort, one can always say that the thing needs a lot of work, because it always does).

Vladimir Nabokov (who, years before, had said to me in his measured way, quite as if it were some kind of straight-faced joke, 'Mr Kubrick is an artist') describes how the hero of *Ada* waits calmly for the morning of the duel in which he is likely to be killed. His stool is, he observes, quite firm. I could only wonder what folly had led me to humiliate myself by delivering myself to the judgement of a man who was hardly renowned for generous responses. Finally, who was Kubrick anyway? He had directed some movies. And he had heard of Vercingetorix. Big deal. The prophylaxis of disparagement began to kick in. The *Spectator* could do it; I could do it. Who cared about writing movies? Where was that bastard Kubrick? Looking for another writer? Let's get that Christmas tree in. Jack Smith usually did it.

F.R.: Telephone!

SYLVIA: Probably Sarah.

F.R.: Can you get it? This damn thing's shedding needles ...

SYLVIA: (Answering the phone) Hello. Oh hello, Stanley. Yes, he is. I'll ... (To F.R.) It's Kubrick.

F.R.: Hello.

S.K.: Freddie?

F.R.: How are you, Stanley?

S.K.: OK, so listen ... I've read the pages and I'm absolutely thrilled.

F.R.: What did you say?

S.K.: I've read the pages. I'm absolutely thrilled.

F.R.: Well, that's ... that's a great relief. I'm ... very glad. Because that means, well, we're on our way. And that first section, well, if I've got that right, the rest ...

S.K.: Are you still working?

F.R.: I've got a little further but they have this thing called Christmas in this country, so we're doing that for the next . . .

S.K.: You're stopping work for Christmas?

F.R.: Aren't you?

S.K.: When are you going to get started again?

F.R.: After the New Year probably.

S.K.: We don't want to lose any time.

F.R.: Do you think we should meet?

S.K.: I can't do Wednesday. How about Thursday?

F.R.: OK, but we're going out to dinner. Can we start early in the day?

S.K.: I'll have them send a car for you. Noon OK?

'Holy shit,' I said, 'he likes it. He actually *likes* it. "Absolutely thrilled." Jesus!'

Sylvia and I held each other, as if in shock. We had been mugged by good news. The two of us have been together since long before my first novel was accepted in 1955 (Sylvia got the news in our basement flat while I was at Crockford's playing bridge). She has endured my rages of disappointment and injustice and she has rejoiced when things went well. Nothing means much to me if I cannot share it with her. Although I scarcely greet success and failure as equal impostors, I always have the consolation, when needed, that my wife is never impressed by the opinions of famous people or divided from me by the things they tell her that she ought to hear about my abrasive persona or unacceptable opinions. She does not care if I make money or if I don't, though neither of us is ashamed if I do.

An enthusiastic reception from the best director in the world never hurt anyone's feelings; I made no apology for enjoying it. What astonished me was the emotion which followed the relief of Stanley's call. Normally, I make my notebooks a repository of anecdotes and precise observations; I try to avoid accounts of my inner feelings. After Kubrick's phone call, however, I was so amazed, and embarrassed, by what I felt that I had recourse to French (in which I am far from reliably fluent) in order to explain what I felt to myself:

'C'est bizarre, ce changement d'esprit qui suit la petite déclaration de S.K. Ma colère est dirigée largement contre moi-même, car – dans le domaine du cinéma – c'est la lâcheté de ma souplesse qui me dégoûte et, après une vingtaine d'années de connivance, me fait réfléchir sur les opportunités ratées ou insuffisamment suivies ou initiées ...'

('It's strange, this change of consciousness which follows S.K.'s little declaration. My anger is directed largely against myself, because – in the realm of the cinema – it's the cowardice of my docility which disgusts me and, after twenty years or so of deference, makes me think back on the opportunities I have missed or insufficiently pursued or failed to instigate ...')

Doubtless, I gave Kubrick's words an oracular sigificance which would have amazed, or alarmed, him. After all, it's a producer/director's job to encourage the troops. There has to be something of the *commander* in anyone who wants to collect both the treasure and the company to make a major movie. A general may be sincere, if it serves his purpose, but his purpose is never sincerity. Kubrick's fascination with autocratic military genius – whether Napoleon or J. Caesar –

may not have been caused by any conscious affinity with them, but he was a man who always dreamed of recruiting grand armies and, cinematically speaking, invading Russia. His films are instinct with violence; Schnitzler's 'love story' culminates in a kind of end-game in which Fridolin and Albertina come, as the US marines used to say, down to the short strokes. Sex and war, in the ancient Greek world (and not only there), shared the same vocabulary.

Ruthlessness and rare talents are seldom far apart. Carlyle defined genius as 'an infinite capacity for taking pains'. There is also a certain willingness to cause them; what mattered to Stanley was not how people felt when they worked with/for him, but what they did, or did not deliver. Long before working with Kubrick, I wrote a short story, *For Joannie*, in which a heartless movie director gets his comeuppance from a female star whose (female) partner he has mistreated. In retrospect, it seems as if I was inoculating myself against just such a man. But there are no such inoculations. My friend Stanley Baron had been quite shocked by *For Joannie*, which he thought, at the time I wrote it, 'unnecessary'. S.B. was my editor at Thames and Hudson when I wrote my biographical studies of Maugham and Byron. I visited him one morning soon after Kubrick had made me so happily angry. Out of loyal reticence, I did not tell S.B. what I was working on, but I did mention that it was originally set in Vienna. He said, 'It's not Schnitzler's *Traumnovelle*, is it?'

The only other person who guessed what the basic material might be was Stanley Donen. He was as generous as usual in wishing me luck in working with 'the best mind in the movies'. He knew that Kubrick had been trying to 'lick' the Schnitzler since before I dined with him, and the others, in Montpelier Square back in 1972. So it happened that the only people (apart from Sylvia) whom I knew for certain to be in the secret were all called Stanley. So what? is right, but there it is.

EXT. STANHOPE GARDENS. LONDON. DAY.

The usual cab from St Albans, with the usual taciturn driver, collects F.R. from his London flat and heads, in winter sunshine, for St Albans. He has two books in his briefcase, Christmas presents for S.K.: the first a book of Greek myths, composed for the Folio Society, with illustrations by Sarah Raphael. The myths have been 'improved' in a variety of styles: the story of Narcissus and Echo is told in *terza rima*; that of Pelops and Hippodameia takes the form of a movie script. That'll teach the great man. The second book is a biography of Julius Caesar.

INT./EXT. CAB. KUBRICK RESIDENCE. DAY.

Can we tell from F.R.'s complacent slump in the back of the cab that he now considers himself less of a probationer than on the first occasion? He smiles at what now seems familiar: the security system, the empty forecourt.

He gets out and goes, without butterflies, to the door which S.K. opens himself, still in the blue overall.

> STANLEY
> Hey. Freddie. How are you?

The white hand is there to be shaken.

> F.R.
> Pretty good.

INT. KUBRICK RESIDENCE. DAY.

STANLEY leads the way through the house in which there are signs of a businesslike Christmas: packages are waiting for despatch. S.K. has a reputation as a present-giver. He is said once to have given an executive a golf cart in order to secure some favour which was not granted.

F.R. follows him, in a relaxed way, to the same long room where, once again, a buffet is waiting.

> STANLEY
> Feel like something to eat?

> F.R.
> I certainly do.

> STANLEY
> We don't want you to have a migraine,
> I mean, do we?

There is a kind of ironic affection in S.K.'s slight smile: he has remembered an intimate detail. F.R. smiles too; he feels a certain affection for the man who had once intimidated him. Perhaps *because* he once intimidated him.

INT. THE LONG ROOM. DAY.

They are eating in the room to which, it seems, no one else has entry. There is no dog in the dog basket.

> STANLEY
> One thing, I really don't want Bill to be
> called Scheuer, OK?

F.R.

It's not a major change.

STANLEY

Give some name that doesn't ...
identify him, OK? It could be
Robinson, but ... we don't want him
to be Jewish.

F.R.

I've clocked that. It doesn't matter to
me, now I'm ... started.

STANLEY

How long did it take you, doing those
pages?

F.R.

Forty years, plus however long it took.

STANLEY

You don't give a lot away, do you?

F.R.

Do you?

STANLEY

Okay.

INT. BILLIARD ROOM. THE SAME. DAY.

F.R. and STANLEY are drinking coffee. STANLEY sits on the
table. F.R. is in a chair. There are no newspapers on the floor.

STANLEY

Do you think we ought to try and ...
plan what happens next?

F.R.
I go on with the script, don't I?

STANLEY
Can you do that without talking in
detail about what's coming?

F.R.
I keep tracking Arthur, and ... like that.
I hate to know ahead of time exactly
what happens. Takes all the life out of
the thing. I'm not someone who wants
to spend his time joining up the dots.

STANLEY
Track Arthur. He knows how to tell a
story.

F.R.
What I don't want to do is write *2010*,
with everything explicit and spelt out.

STANLEY
Did I ask you to do that?

F.R.
You never know what's going to be
suggested by a story until you get to a
given point. I don't want to *just* track
Arthur. I hope you don't want me to.

Is F.R. angling for a statement of confidence from S.K. that he
invents what seems good to him, in the light of that first
forty-two pages? If so, he is disappointed.

STANLEY

I don't want to have too long a wait
before I get another chunk, okay?

F.R.

Soon as it's ready, you'll have it.

STANLEY

I don't have to wait till you've done
another forty, do I?

F.R.

You know what this is like, don't you,
for me? It's like submitting a new script
every damn time.

STANLEY

I know. But do I?

F.R.

As soon as I've done enough to make
sense as a sequence, I won't hold it up.
But I can't go scene by scene before I
even know what's relevant, how one
scene hooks up with another.
Shakespeare didn't write 'to be' and
then make sure the director liked it
before he went on to write 'or not to be'.

STANLEY

Did I ask you to do anything like that?

F.R.

I've had some experiences.

                    STANLEY
We've all had experiences. Is this an
experience?

                      F.R.
It's fine.

                    STANLEY
We need to find a way of doing the orgy
scene. When you get to that, I think
we should talk over some ideas.
Because . . .

                      F.R.
What's there reads fine, in its way, but
it won't play, will it? It's a little bit too
Busby Berkeley.

                    STANLEY
You ever go to an orgy?

                      F.R.
I was asked. Almost. I was working on
a film with a director on location and
word came down that there was an orgy
being set up in some suite upstairs in
the hotel. I asked him if he was tempted
to go and he said, yes, he was, wasn't
I? I said that maybe the reason I wasn't
was that he was. How about you?

                    STANLEY
How about whorehouses?

F.R.

Too scared, probably. I grew up in
wartime London. They had these
posters everywhere: Clean Living Is The
Only Safeguard.

STANLEY

So, what else is there we have to talk
about?

F.R.

I don't have a lot.

STANLEY

How soon am I going to get something?
You'll start right in after New Year's,
right?

F.R.

Or earlier. Was my plan.

STANLEY

Sounds like a good one.

F.R.

Have a good Christmas.

STANLEY

I'll try. One of the dogs is sick. Could
be diabetes. But I'll try. Ten pages is
plenty, if you want to send them. I like
to know what's going on.

F.R. senses that S.K. is a man trapped in his own web. He is an
Odysseus, longing for wider experiences but unable to shake
off his own timidities and obliged to ask others about what

he wishes he knew, or had happened to, himself. He is the sedentary wandering Jew, rootlessly rooted within his own defences.

> F.R.
> Well ...

> STANLEY
> You want me to call you a taxi?

> F.R.
> If ...

> STANLEY
> We're on our way, aren't we?

> F.R.
> If you say so.

While STANLEY punches in the numbers, F.R. unbuckles his briefcase and takes out the books.

> F.R.
> Coupla things might amuse you.

> STANLEY
> He won't be a coupla minutes.

Somehow, F.R. wants to smile at the constraint which keeps two men of their age somehow wary of each other. But the wariness is there, as well as the regret that it is.

When Tony Frewin, who was delegated to call me, sometimes, with messages from Stanley, kindly told Sylvia that my chunk of script had given the people in the Kubrick camp 'the best Christmas they'd had in eighteen years', his genial remark had the effect of rekindling my almost inexplicable fury.

I had promised to meet a TV executive, Ms M., who said that she *might* want an unperformed script of mine for a series of films she had set up at the BBC. *The Evening and the Morning* was not being added to those definitely selected, but I just might be on the bench. Since my son Paul would be my producer, I agreed to discuss the script at a café in Soho.

I went first to see one of my London agents, Jane Annakin, who was in the Marsden Hospital, suffering like her partner, Roger Williams, from cancer. She talked so calmly in her beautiful voice that she might have had a slight malaise from which she would soon be better. How shameful it was to have to look at my watch!

I arrived at the café in Wardour Street without knowing what Ms M. looked like. A woman, standing at one of those odious high tables without chairs which encourage customers to drink their coffee and be gone, beckoned to me with one finger, like a teacher singling out a backward pupil whom she suspects of not having done his prep. Usually, I try to be very diplomatic and charming at such meetings, though not everyone always finds me so. On this occasion, Ms M.'s instructive condescensions contrasted so sharply with Kubrick's praise that I could not contain my sarcasm.

When I discovered that she had never even *heard* of *Les Valseuses*, perhaps the best French film of the Seventies, I offered to send it to her. It was never too late, I said, to begin one's education in the cinema. She left without swearing to promote me to her first team.

Paul had been embarrassed and was loudly angry with me. We had a wretched lunch trying to talk calmly about the adaptation of *The Thought Gang*, a novel by Tibor Fischer on which we had bought an option. I have rarely bought 'properties' but I had liked Tibor, when he came to me for advice as a young man, and I had nominated his first novel,

Under the Frog, as a *Sunday Times* book of the year. *The Thought Gang* had a few very good scenes and a lot of quite amusing, parodic philo-verbiage. I intended to do a spec script of it after I was done with Mr K. When Paul asked how long that was likely to mean, I said, 'Well, how long can the script be? A hundred and forty pages, tops. So . . . end of February, I should be pretty well there. If things go on the way they're going.'

Notebook entry: 'This Christmas is proving a season of deaths. Roger Williams, who stayed with Jane and their daughter at our French house, has gone, and Jack Smith is now, it seems, dying. Peter May too is dead. Was he a cricketing genius? When I was at Charterhouse, he scored centuries in almost every match. I once had lunch with him, when he was thinking of writing his memoirs. I asked him how he could decide, when a good spin-bowler was bowling to him, whether he was going to get a googly or a leg-break. He said that he couldn't. Then what did he do? "Hit the ball before it matters which way it's going to break." Genius simplifies. Only modest players, and artists, entertain a huge range of possible responses. Kubrick (I have to hope) is waiting for the right ball to hit. The others don't interest him. Will he make this picture? Tony Frewin says that he certainly will. How much does Frewin know? We shall see.'

I went to a meeting at John Schlesinger's new apartment in Gloucester Road, round the corner from our London flat. Antoine de Clermont-Tonnerre, one of the producers of *Cloud on Sand* (what the *hell* did it mean?), was over from Paris. Paul and I had had a meeting with him on another project in his very grand apartment in an *hôtel particulier* in the 16th *arrondissement*. We were with him for an hour or so, during which he did not offer us so much as a glass of water. I said how glad I was to see him again. I was then invited to tell him and John what I thought needed to be done to make *Cloud on Sand* into a movie. Even when screenwriters do people a favour, they can be made to feel that they are auditioning. I performed, as T. E. Hulme once wrote, 'like any creeping Turk to the Bosphorus', though with a measure of asperity. I conceded that the novel might have been brilliantly reviewed (so the dust-jacket announced), but warned them that it was so completely without merit that only Marty's friendship with the author could explain his advocacy of it.

Out of friendship for John, I agreed – quite as if I needed a job – to write a few pages outlining my ideas of how to beef up the plot. My diplomatic motive was that I still wanted John to commit to directing my script of *Armed Response*, the little TV movie which, the producers had recently declared, to John's displeasure, absolutely *had* to be shot in Toronto.

During Christmas, I composed a five-page, single-spaced letter for John to send to Marty, setting out how I thought the cloud could be detached from the sand. It always amuses me to render unnecessarily generous services. I once did something similar for Jo Janni, the producer of *Darling* and *Far from the Madding Crowd*, whose recent death John and I and others, including the still remarkably beautiful Julie Christie, commemorated at the Italian Cultural Centre that same season. Once, when I refused to accept Jo's proposed elaborate 'tax-free' – i.e. illegal – means of payment, for a petty rewrite, and offered to do the work for nothing, Jo said, 'Fred, in many ways nothing is too much.'

John's secretary telephoned acknowledgement of my letter. Neither he nor Marty Scorsese ever thanked me for it. Despite the Canadian locations, John did undertake to direct my little TV film, but he dumped it at the last minute when a hotter ticket presented itself. Of course I understood.

Stanley presented me with a magnificent two-volume boxed, professionally wrapped, edition of Van Gogh's paintings.

S.K.: Freddie, can you talk?

F.R.: Oh yes.

S.K.: Happy New Year.

F.R.: You too.

S.K.: So . . . how goes it?

F.R.: Not bad.

S.K.: Did you see the new Woody Allen yet?

F.R.: *Husbands and Wives*? Yes, I did. I liked it. Except for the bilious beginning. Did you?

S.K.: Pretty good movie. Did you notice something?

F.R.: What?

S.K.: The size of that apartment they lived in? Guy's supposed to be some kind of a book editor or something and they live in this huge apartment. Notice how wide that hallway was? Nice for moving cameras through but a little expensive for a guy who works for a publisher. We'd better not make that mistake. You know what a doctor like Bill makes today in New York City?

F.R.: No, I don't. A hundred and fifty grand?

S.K.: Just don't make the apartment too big. They wouldn't have anybody living in. Maybe a help. Don't make her Spanish.

F.R.: OK. Why not?

S.K.: We're going to have to think about that orgy scene. I mean, what happens out there in that house? Arthur doesn't tell us a lot.

F.R.: No. The way it's written, it's sort of a blue musical. The Rockettes with no pants on. I was reading some stuff about an orgy the other day.

S.K.: Some book you're reviewing?

F.R.: Want me to send it to you?

S.K.: Anything that might be useful. So, listen ... don't wait too long before you send me some pages. A dozen at a time is fine. I don't want us to get on the wrong track. And, I've been thinking, maybe those first forty should come down to a lot fewer.

F.R.: That's what I said when I wrote to you.

S.K.: So, would you ... do that? And keep telling me as much as you can about everything.

January 1995. (FAX) FOR STANLEY KUBRICK

On October 31st, 1501, the Duke of Valentino threw a notorious sex party in the Vatican, which Pope Alexander VI attended:

'In the evening a supper was given in the Duke of Valentino's apartment in the Apostolic palace, with fifty respectable prostitutes, called courtesans, in attendance. After supper they danced with the servants and others present, at first in their clothes and then naked. Later candelabra with lighted candles were taken from the tables and put on the floor and chestnuts were scattered around them. The prostitutes crawled naked on their hands and knees between the candelabra, picking up the chestnuts. The Pope, the Duke, and his sister Donna Lucrezia, were all present to watch. Finally, prizes of silk doublets, shoes, hats and other clothes were offered to the men who copulated with the greatest number of prostitutes. According to those who were present, this performance took place in the public hall (that is, the Sala Regia, used for public consistories).'

This comes from Richard Sennett's *Flesh and Stone*, and the quotation is from Georgina Masson's *Courtesans of the Italian Renaissance*.

I want to use this as the basis for a 'role-playing' game which will give shape and sequence to the visit to the Long Island party at which 'Nightingale' will play, as in the master-text. I imagine you are familiar with the role-playing craze which has led to several deaths in France recently, especially among teenagers. What happens is, roughly, that a band of friends take on the characters of comic-strip figures – the comic strip is often both 'Gothic' and grown-up/erotic in France – and when they meet, resume the story so far. On occasions, this 'game' goes so far that people leave their real worlds and become inhabitants of the 'other world' in which they have often dangerous fantasy identities, which may lead to murder or (more often) suicide. I think that this could work *à la merveille* – marvellously, as they might say at Warners – for us. Any explanation can be given by Nightingale, before *and* after the event. The advantage for us is that it is both a game (hence Bill can play and then leave without feeling a total coward) *and* a counterfeit reality in which the 'countess's' death might be the consequence of, well, taking it all too seriously. *Please* believe that this need not be 'too complicated' (I'll make it clear, or clearer, as required), because it gives us a central 'drama' within the story, a true dream, as it were, which fits perfectly with Arthur's scheme and yet makes it (much) better.

I know it may *seem* risky, but that is what I like about it. It will give Bill that feeling which we all – don't we? – know so well in a dream when everyone else is rehearsed and ready to take part in a play and we do not know what to say or do and yet must seem calm and in no need of 'the book'. Believe me, maestro, this gives a vibrant centre to the story.

It might have been less embarrassing not to cite this fax, to which Stanley responded without enthusiasm. Its almost tutorial tone derived, I suppose, from the confidence excited by his response to my first forty pages. I suffered from the conceit of imagining that I had qualified as his genuine collaborator and that I could contribute not only to the script but also to the conception of the movie. Provided they can take credit for it, most directors are glad of the fertility of writers. I had a feeling, which was not to prove erroneous, that Kubrick did not really know what kind of *story* he was intending to tell. What interested him was the atmosphere of eroticism and the distinct sexuality of conjugal love. He talked of casting a couple who were married in real life, perhaps Kim Basinger and Alec Baldwin. The orgy was a sweet opportunity to make the kind of elegant blue movie that he had once talked about with Terry Southern, whose novel *Candy* (written with Mason Hoffenberg) Dick Zanuck sent to me when we were living in Rome. Dick said that he had heard that I knew how it could be done. He had heard wrong. *Candy* was a catchpenny and silly Sixtiesish skit on pornography. I remember only a scene in which the heroine excitedly asks a hunchback dwarf to fuck her with his hump. I was sceptical of the anatomical practicality of this exercise; still less could I imagine it in a movie.

S.K.: Terry and I had an office out at Pinewood when we were working on the script of *Doctor Strangelove*. Down the corridor Romy Schneider had her dressing-room for something she was doing out there. She kinda pissed us off because she never said hello or anything. She'd walk right past in the corridor with her nose in the air. Terry was smoking a lot of weed, you know, and he ... decided to do something about this stuck-up attitude. So he said, why don't we write her a love letter? He wrote her this letter and what it said was, 'If you want to get some head, it's room 221.' That's the room we were working in. He went and stuck it under her dressing-room door.

F.R.: Did she want any?

S.K.: Not while I was around.

F.R.: *Strangelove* was the best.

S.K.: A lotta people hated it.

F.R.: That must've pleased you.

S.K.: What do you mean? They thought I was a traitor. They damn near refused to show it in the theatres.

F.R.: You'd made your point though.

S.K.: A lot of people didn't even want to show it. We started out to make a serious movie, you know that, don't you? But we found we couldn't. Terry and I ... we'd sit in there and ... you couldn't take this stuff seriously. But it *was* serious.

F.R.: Sellers was unbelievable. How did you get him to do that stuff? Was it all scripted?

S.K.: He just did it. Know what I did? He was so great. But he couldn't do it over. Once or twice, that was it. So what I did was, I set up like six cameras. First thing in the morning, Peter'd come in and he'd say when he was ready and I just let him do what he wanted to do.

F.R.: I knew him when he was only known on the radio. A BBC producer said to me, 'Isn't it lucky there's a medium where an actor can perform without being seen, because Peter is so ugly he could never get a job acting in public.'

S.K.: I'd let him go on until he said that was it and then we'd cover the scene.

F.R.: Jesus, the moment when he said '*Mein Führer*, I can walk!'! Did you script that?

S.K.: Have you seen *Pulp Fiction*?

F.R.: Yes, I have. I liked it a lot. Did you?

S.K.: It's something we have to take into account, I think.

F.R.: How do we do that? Have them all say fuck a lot?

S.K.: The way it was told.

F.R.: I liked it, but our story doesn't need a loop in it like that, does it?

S.K.: The pace. Watch the pace.

Having, it seemed, given Stanley the first act he wanted, I resumed the script with little hesitation or anxiety. I even dared to decorate it with a witty remark or two. For instance, I had the dead senator's daughter say of her father that even when he was clearly dying he kept saying how much better he felt. 'He was a true politician,' she told Bill. 'He figured that as long as he could tell lies there had to be hope.'

When it came to the scene with the prostitute, I thought I had to diverge from Arthur's *gemütlich* tone. As he reveals in his memoirs, he had a soft spot for the young whores of Vienna who had been forced into a life of degradation. As a sixteen-year-old, he tells us, he tried to 'redeem' the naked girl who had stretched herself in front of him, little expecting her beardless client to turn into a moralizing lecturer. Not believing that such a '*süsse Madel*' (sweet thing) was likely to be found around Time Square, I upgraded Bill's hooker into a more aggressive, modern and commercial character. My New York whore was quick-tongued rather than shy, more demanding than wistful (Schnitzler's girl was so touched by Fridolin's gentlemanliness that she decided not to go out again that night). My gimme-the-money babe was, I thought, a plausible, if not a literal, translation.

S.K.: Freddie? Can you talk?

F.R.: Of course.

S.K.: OK, so . . . I got the new pages. Are you OK?

F.R.: Tell me.

S.K.: It's only natural, and inevitable, as we go ahead . . . I'll maybe have more things I'll want to . . . talk about . . .

F.R.: Sure.

S.K.: Because I don't like the scene with the hooker. I mean, she sounds like she's Barbra Streisand, know what I mean? Doing the New York hooker. The dialogue kinda goes boom-boom and a boom-boom, which I don't . . . I don't want that. How about we just follow Arthur?

F.R.: We're talking about New York City today. I just don't

believe there are a lot of sentimental hookers on the streets.

S.K.: You do that New York dialogue boom-boom and a boom-boom and I don't want that. Just follow Arthur's beats is what I want you to do. And another thing . . . you know that scene where Bill and the other guy walk away down the street. You say they're talking. What're they talking about?

F.R.: It's the end of the scene and they're a long way from the camera. I just meant . . . you know . . . they behave like friends do . . .

S.K.: So what are they talking about?

F.R.: I don't know. What would you like them to? They're a couple of doctors, right, so what do doctors talk about? Golf; the stock market; the tits on that nurse who's on nights; ah . . . holidays . . .

S.K.: Couple of Gentiles, right?

F.R.: That's what you wanted them to be.

S.K.: Coupla Jews, what do we know about what those people talk about when they're by themselves?

F.R.: Stanley, come *on*, those people! You've heard them talking. They talk about much the same kind of things we talk about, *don't they*? I mean, you've heard them, haven't you, at the next table in restaurants, in front of you in theatres, and ah places? I have and . . .

S.K.: Maybe, but I'll tell you something: they always know you're there.

F.R.: Stanley, you know something? You're such a paranoid

you make me feel completely normal. You don't really *mean* that, do you?

S.K.: The Holocaust, what do you think?

F.R.: What do I think? I think we probably don't have time just now ...

S.K.: As a subject for a movie. Can it be done?

F.R.: It's been done a few times, hasn't it?

S.K.: Has it? I didn't know that.

F.R.: Did you ever see a movie that Munk did – half-did – called *The Passenger*?

S.K.: Wasn't that Antonioni? With Jack in it.

F.R.: The Munk came first. I'm surprised you don't know it. Because it had a lot of stills in it. Not because he wanted it to, but because he died half-way through and he had story-boarded the whole movie with stills from scenes he had in his head. When they did the assembly, they put the stills in where they thought he wanted them to go, but no one knew what *exactly* they were meant to convey, or what they were part of. So you got a movie sequence followed by a still or two, or three, and then it went back into movement, and so on. Very enigmatic finally. I think, as I recall, it was about a woman who recognizes a man on a cruise she is going on, long after the war, as one of the sadistic guards in a camp she was in. There were wonderful scenes in the movie. And extraordinary economy. For instance, a scene where a man is leading a cart, pulled by a horse, out of a yard. The cart has very, very high sides, made of wooden planks. You can't tell what it contains. But you can guess. And then the carter takes a long stick, with a Y at the end, and reaches up with it and the Y is used to fork a single dead white arm which is hanging over the side. It pushes it up and back into oblivion behind the planks and you realize that the cargo this man is wheeling out of the yard is a heap of corpses. Also . . .

S.K.: OK, so what else is there?

F.R.: *Nuit et Brouillard*. Which was a sort of documentary, but . . .

S.K.: Anything else?

F.R.: (Knowing damn well what he is being urged to get to) Well, there's *Schindler's List*. Isn't there?

S.K.: Think that was about the Holocaust?

F.R.: Wasn't it? What else was it about?

S.K.: That was about success, wasn't it? The Holocaust is about six million people who get killed. *Schindler's List* was about six hundred people who don't. Anything else?

When Stanley died, few of the obituaries mentioned that he was a Jew. There was, perhaps, a kind of tact in this. In the pre-war Austro-Hungarian world from which his family – like Arthur Schnitzler's – sprang, Jewishness was considered so shameful a condition that Gentiles were in the habit of saying, not least of those whom they admired, *'Il est – pardon! – Juif.'* It is, however, absurd to try to understand Stanley Kubrick without reckoning on Jewishness as a fundamental aspect of his mentality, if not of his work in general.

He himself was known to have said that he was not really a Jew, he just happened to have two Jewish parents. Jews are not featured in any of his films; he seemed to expose, or at least to dwell on, many ugly aspects of human behaviour, but he never confronted anti-Semitism. Is it unduly fanciful to see fear and horror driving him to face in art the malice which he dreaded in life? The great thing about violence in films, however scandalous, is that the director at least is in control of it. He can toy with brutality, brutally, without it hurting *him*.

Stanley did try, for some time, to develop a novel by Louis Begley, *Wartime Lies*, into a movie, but he never, as they say, licked it. Begley's novel is terse and, I believe, authentic; it tells of an aunt and her nephew who survive the Nazis (and others) by a series of subterfuges which finally turn them into adepts of fraudulence. Its routines of evasive deception must have appealed to Stanley; he maintained his unique standing in the movies by the creation of an elusive persona whom no one, not even studio heads, cared (or, finally, dared) to challenge. In some ways, I suspect, he was a timid man with little appetite for the battles which so intrigued him. His need to protect himself, as far as possible, from criticism or intrusion suggested some sublime paranoia which demanded that he be spared the inquisitive prattle of journalists and the jostling of sycophants. 'Coupla Jews, what do we know . . .?' We could know many things, but never what 'those people' were really like, when they were alone and planning all kinds of murderous things. What could be known was how they *looked*, how they moved, how they *acted*, whatever was not going on in the unfathomable secrecy of their heads. Kubrick soon lost interest in the analysis of characters. How could he ever be sure about those alien thought-processes or even their sentiments? Love was never his theme, though desire – not least for money – went right back to his earliest work. He never began to inquire whether Bill or Alice 'really' loved each other. How would we know? And who cares? Spelling things out, like sincerity, was of no interest to him; it led to explicit horrors such as *2010*, in which the audience got told what was 'really' going on. Kubrick's crackers carried no motto.

Mid-January 1995. Journal entry: 'When he calls, I have the feeling that he is making sure that I am still on the job. *Almost* as if apologizing, he told me about the supervisors at MGM when he was a contract writer and had to punch a clock in and out. He laughed at the absurdity of the factory schedule and *almost* conceded that he was playing the checker's part with me. As if to prove what buddies we now are, he uses the word "cunt" a lot. He talked of a "shaggy-cunt story" when I outlined my role-playing scenario for the orgy. He reverts constantly to the big scene at the party. I cannot imagine that *scripting* can supply what he wants, but he wants it scripted and keeps asking me to think about it.'

Kubrick's myth has generated the idea that he was somehow exempt from the usual travails of apprenticeship. In fact, and unsurprisingly, he too endured rejections and humiliation. When he was working, wretchedly, at MGM as a writer, which was never what he wanted or even imagined himself to be, he tried to develop original ideas that he could direct. One of them he sent to Gregory Peck, a great star in those days. If he hoped for encouragement, he did not receive it. 'Know what happened? He sent it back with a note saying that I shouldn't write that kind of material, or send it to him. Like I'd insulted him, y'know?'

I never asked Stanley what movies he had written for MGM. It is unlikely any of them ever got made or that he would want credit for them if they did. He hung out with other young hopefuls in 1950s Hollywood. One of his buddies, R.P., later became a television producer. During this time, Stanley discovered a novel by Lionel White, called *Clean Break*, from which he contrived *The Killing*, his first movie to excite critical and professional attention.

Although unmistakably a B-picture, and made on a small budget, *The Killing* was original both in the articulation of time and in the variety of viewpoints. As became typical of Kubrick, it was savagely skittish: the clown masks which the villains wore for their heist only later became a cliché. The gang of droogs in *A Clockwork Orange* had something of the same brutal levity. The sour twist in *The Killing* was, of course, that it was a *horse* that got murdered. It was a sweetly callous defeat of routine expectation. Only when I worked with Stanley did I come to know with what peculiar tenderness he regarded animals. Even Warner Brothers executives have tears in their eyes when they describe how devoted he was to his mallards.

The grittiness of the settings in *The Killing*, like Sterling Hayden's resigned nobility, as his last hope of a fortune literally blew away, transcended the B-picture genre (later venerated by *Cahiers du Cinéma*) to which the movie belonged. Kubrick's first unmistakably Kubrickian movie made the young director the target of several offers. As usual in such cases, not all his buddies were whole-heartedly delighted. R.P. said to him, 'Why are you getting all these calls suddenly? The only difference between you and me is *The Killing*.'

Kubrick remembered slights with more accuracy than he did flattery, and with vindictive rancour. R.P., he told me, was a guy who, when he could afford it, used to have a hooker come by the house at six in the evening and have sex with him, before he went out on a date, in case he didn't manage to get laid that night. Like Schnitzler's hero, S.K. was fascinated and appalled by things he witnessed but could not quite bring himself to do. The voyeur thinks to keep himself clean by only *seeing* what other people are capable of doing.

Stanley had Tony Frewin send me a batch of Helmut Newton's erotic photographs in order, I suppose, to prime my imagination. It was curious (and appetizing) how many of them featured women fondling other women. Yet when, in one of the scenes between Alice and Bill, I had her ask him if he had ever imagined her being a boy, Stanley rejected the exchange with something like disgust. Newton's photographs were divided between fantasies, set in extremely elegant surroundings, and shots of whorish women in the style of stills from low-life documentaries. Sometimes the desire to be perverse became comic: one shameless brunette, rising from a rumpled bed, bent her seductive smile on the photographer although she was leaning on a black cane, wearing a neckbrace and a cast on her left leg. Newton seemed obsessed (or hoped that his public would be) by male voyeurism: his composite pictures often featured a naked woman or women – shaggy-cunt pictures indeed – being watched by evening-dressed males. The shamelessness of the women was in contrast to the furtive dignity of the men who watched them (not a prick in sight).

The women often wore heels when they wore nothing else. Their shamelessness exemplified, it seemed, the liberation of penis-less bondage; they had nothing to hide, and did not hide it. One of the oddest photographs was of a slim, full-breasted naked woman bending over to apply lipstick to a seated man in a decorous suit (but loosened tie). He was looking elsewhere than at her conical breasts. He might have been at the dentist's.

Besides the photographs, I received a bundle of reproductions of paintings and drawings by both Egon Schiele and Gustave Klimt, with all of which, I assured Stanley, I was familiar. If I appreciated the deluge of erotic largesse, was it likely to contribute anything much to what would better emerge from Schnitzler or from my (and S.K.'s) imagination? Did S.K. really want the look of his movie to ape Newton? Surely it would be unwise to search for solutions outside what Schnitzler's myth itself suggested. Was it misguided modesty in Stanley that led him sometimes to seek chic answers in other people's work? The weakest thing in *A Clockwork Orange* was the décor of the opening sequence, featuring a café furnished with plastic tables in the form of naked women in S/M gear. It was commissioned from a trendy designer of the Seventies and now serves only to anchor the movie in a period in which it was never intended to take place. Helmut Newton *had* to be irrelevant to our movie.

I worked on steadily, sending Stanley pages, until at a certain point, I suggested that I drive right on through to the end, so that we could at least see what we'd got. He agreed. A few weeks later, I was able to write in my notebook as follows:

'*Ouf!* I have written THE END after 172 pages, having completed a petty, yet substantial, work of translation. I have no illusions about having created a work of art, but there's no shortage of artfulness. It may yet provide material for something amazing, although it can never be amazing by itself: either he eventually makes the movie or I've wasted my time. I have a feeling of escape and deprivation which echoes Bill's emotions when he escaped from his own dream. S.K. has become less remote. He seems now to have some kind of wary dependence on me, if not on my collaboration (he doesn't want to make anything *with* anybody).

'The screenwriter plays the traditional woman's part; he can be divorced (like an orthodox Jewess) with a single phrase, and has no appeal. (I think orthodox Jews have to say "I divorce you" three times, which is more gracious than producers usually bother to be.) There is a kind of freedom in such "feminine" subjection; something like Kipling's whore, the screenwriter has duties without responsibilities.

'I cannot predict, even now, whether S.K. will like my new pages (I have broken all my rules and sent him chunks, and rewritten and rewritten them, up until the last rush of pages) or whether, if he does, he will not – as contractually he certainly can – appropriate them and send me, gratefully or not, on my way. My sentimental guess is that he welcomes my conversation no less than my dialogue, but who knows? S.K. is unique in his talent and in his capacity to retain the respect of men who, normally, respect nothing and no one, but that cannot protect him from the contagion of ruthlessness; it may even make it a part of his defence against crass intrusion (he keeps his fences in *very* good repair, even if he always – so far – picks up for me).

'Am I inside or outside? What further use is he likely to make of me? And does it matter? Vanity, careerism and greed jostle at the bend. I should like to see this movie made, both because S.K. *is* a genius, at least of a kind, and because I might then be liberated to create better films; it would be a small triumph if the film is made, if only (as is probable) with my name adjacent to S.K.'s. I know nothing of his hopes and intentions. I cannot even be sure whether, when I tell myself that I like him, I feel affection, interest or merely hopeful relief that he seems to like me, and what I have done. He grows less remarkable as he becomes less guarded; however, he is still the hero, and I am still his valet. I should like to think that I am proving an independently-minded Figaro, but I am there to serve and whatever is not to his taste, however much *I* like it, has to be removed. He has become more trusting, however, if never unwary. Yesterday he described a consultant surgeon as "a pin-striped *goy*".'

While I waited for Stanley to respond to the fat volume of pages I had sent him, I toyed with another story for the secret *decalogue* which I liked to think he might do one day. It was drawn from a *fait-divers* in the French press. A young man was accused of rape, in Marseilles, on circumstantial evidence, and convicted. My friend, the Hellenist Pierre Vidal-Naquet, and others formed a committee of support for the imprisoned youth, who seemed to have been railroaded. Their efforts were successful; the conviction was quashed. Thus vindicated, the young man came out of prison and almost immediately raped an American student. This time, the evidence left no doubt about his guilt. I could imagine Kieslowski, or Kubrick, making a savagely neat hour out of such an ironic story (perhaps the young man began to wish that he was the rapist he was falsely accused of being). If my completed script received the same response as those first forty pages, I might be able to resume work on my *decalogue* before the end of February.

It did not. The surge of enthusiasm which had carried me to such copiousness was not appreciated. Stanley was neither grateful nor reproachful. I had been like a Penelope who had decided to complete the tapestry and to hell with it. S.K. was simply not interested in any romantic rush of inspiration. He could never, I now realize, be interested in my contributing anything *outstanding* to his film; what was manifestly mine would detract from him (he had been exasperated by Terry Southern's claims to having written *Doctor Strangelove*, though he never denied that Terry had done valuable work). When Stanley called, he suggested with no more than a sigh that I go back to the point where he thought things had got out of control (which meant, of course, out of *his* control). I was more disappointed than surprised; I saw no qualitative difference between the first section, which he still admired, and the last, which he dismissed. However, it was not worth arguing about; he was bound to be right, or at least the boss, even if he was wrong.

No crisis of conscience was involved; Sisyphus is defined by his rock-rolling. I sighed and rolled mine all the way up the hill again. This time I submitted clutches of pages to S.K. in order to avoid any enthusiastic jump to conclusions. In any other circumstances, I should almost certainly have insisted that, having written a fat script (with all the novelistic detail requested), I had fully discharged my contractual obligations so far as 'the first draft' was concerned. What he was asking for was a further draft under the rubric of the first. I did not argue, less out of cowardice than because I had resolved to stick with Kubrick to the end, if I could. I agreed to go again to St Albans in order to consult over whatever changes had to be made to the changes before S.K. would concede that a first draft had been completed. We did not speak directly about the contractual specifics, but both of us knew that I was near the end of the first length of rope by which I was attached to the project.

March 1995. Notebook entry: 'S.K. had a buffet lunch waiting for when I visited him on the first two occasions. Last Saturday he was less generous; he received me in the billiard room with two piles of tuna-fish sandwiches, one with margarine and one without, both with crusts. His wife was having a silk-screen printing session which had drawn a number of local friends with Range Rovers and Mercedes. We drank a jug of white wine and, in due course, coffee which was served by a blonde American girl with no speaking part.

'I had small memory of S.K.'s appearance (it is as if he

scarcely has one) except for the small white elegance of his delicate hands, the fingers often splayed to their limit as he gestures with them. They seem to announce a different personality (all that is left of the tender Kubrick), detached from the hard, tough world of the movies. They are unblistered and unbarnacled by Hollywood in-fighting. (There was a famous Spanish princess who, as she grew older, believed that her arms were still unblemished by age and allowed the court painter no glimpse of any other part of her person.)

'The blue-jeaned costume and the rumpledness of the "public" persona could be an approximation – even a kind of scapegoat – to the evasive personality within. S.K. does not propose to be judged, or even *revealed*. He is either too bitter or too intelligent to have a purpose or a policy. It is enough to conceive of masterpieces, or to parade as fabrication aspects of what he may think to be the truth. Meaning? Under the guise of success-seeking, he hopes to smuggle the contraband of the truth into his soiled medium, film, the only one in which he can hope to sustain his reputation as an artist. He has immense curiosity, but lacks the confidence which might organize it into knowledge. He also affects the meticulousness of the academics on whose lectures he once sat in (not being a scholar, he wishes – as a scholar does – to check and check, so that his errors never emerge). His loneliness comes of pressure from two sides: he may be a genius, but he fears to look a fool. He is innocent enough, in some ways, to be both.

'He told me, quite seriously, that he could *always* appear to be able to speak French by saying, "Cat-oo-dee". I was puzzled and asked him to repeat the magic phrase. He repeated, "Cat-oo-dee", as if he was beginning to doubt whether I knew any French at all. I said, "Oh my God, you mean *qu'as-tu dit?*" "That's right: Cat-oo-dee." I was about to warn him that it was not wise to say *"tu"* to everyone in France, but Stanley Kubrick probably could.

'It is difficult for me to have a relationship with such a man, perhaps with anybody, without wishing upon him those sympathetic qualities which will allow me to believe that, *grosso modo*, we have much in common. I have to think that he believes that I have greater cinematic vision than any old hired help. His early applause seemed to indicate that such recognition was *chose faite*. I had, after all, been the first to be unguarded, when I allowed him to know how excited I was to work with him. When he said that *he* was "thrilled", it seemed that our alliance had become symmetrical. Since I never claimed, even to myself, that the fat script I sent him was "right", I have no cause to resent its reception. What is a little sad, this gloomy March morning, is the sense I have (and probably should always have had) that he does not want, and never wanted, a *collaborator*, but rather a skilled mechanic who can crank out the dross he will later turn to gold.'

The difficulty with proceeding more or less scene by scene, as Stanley wanted, was not only that I was on a treadmill. More significantly for the movie, so much attention was being paid to the trees that we were giving no clear shape to the wood. Jean-Luc Godard had mocked the old Aristotelian principle when he said that of course there had to be a beginning, a middle and an end, but not necessarily in that order. He had not proved the principle pointless. I remained convinced that there had, for instance, to be a link between the scene at the party at the beginning of the movie and the orgy and its consequences. Otherwise there would be a concatenation of events, but neither progression nor effective closure. Schnitzler's 'Dream Novella' lacked any neat explanation because to explain a dream is to rationalize it. However, since Stanley did not want the movie to be nothing *but* a dream, it seemed essential to give it cohesion.

I argued that it was a mistake to introduce the character of Ziegler, as I proposed to call him (in unaffectionate memory of 'Ziggy', a garrulous agent who once represented me in California), at the beginning of the piece and never again to meet either him or the half-naked girl whom Bill treats upstairs. Stanley jeered at my appetite for plotted neatness, but I returned to the charge, once again in vain, when I went to see him. Had the movie been an original screenplay of mine (in which case I doubt if Kubrick would have been interested in it), I should have had a stronger voice in the matter. As it was, I could persist, but never insist. The difference between writing books and writing scripts was never more manifest than in those days of my enforced conformity with Arthur Schnitzler's 'plot'.

I began to fear that Kubrick might make another movie like *Full Metal Jacket*, in which the brilliant elements failed to bond into unity. Was he going to be so determined to confound routine expectations that that was all he did? The denial of conclusive satisfaction to the audience would be a twist without savour. Obedient dissidence was my only available response. In the days that followed, I wrote, and rewrote, and reverted tactfully to my point that the movie could not end as mysteriously as it began without leaving a sense of frustration. Kubrick listened but he did not yet change his point of view. 'Stick with Arthur's beats' was a fundamentalism which, for the moment, embargoed invention.

The principle was that I was free to do things again, but not to do them freely. Stanley was attentive to my pages, and alert to what he did not like, but he admitted that he was making no contribution: 'I wish I could give you some input, but I can't. I'm not a writer.'

He seemed not very interested in words. He might admire the sharpness of my dialogue, but it was not something he wanted to *film*, and film alone was his art form. He often urged me to use Voice Over to establish what might otherwise require more dialogue than he wanted. The great advantage of Voice Over for a director such as Kubrick, who cared more for images than for drama, was that a narrator imposed no preconceived scheme on what took place in the frame. Stanley favoured Voice Over because it avoided all need to use dialogue to articulate how people felt or what motives they had. The narrator could state quite bluntly what it irked Kubrick to have to have the characters reveal in speech. The artist always wants to minimize whatever aspects of his medium impede him from using the available space for what he regards as the heart of the matter. Kubrick wanted to *show*, not tell. He preferred to leave motive or 'psychology' to be divined by the spectator. What he 'meant' was never explicit. Ambiguity left him free but not responsible.

I came slowly to realize that not only did he want no jokes, he was not even eager that the characters should have any particular personality: he would as soon have types as individuals with specific histories (my credit sequence, suggesting the Freudian background of Bill's character, was soon axed). He did not want the scenes to carry any authorial mark but his. If I was preparing the way for him to do his stuff, anything that was markedly *mine* was never the stuff he was going to do.

His patience was both polite and implacable: I could see no end to it. The writer on a movie is like someone running the first leg of a relay race. He has to set off at full speed while everyone else stands around and wonders if it is going to be worth their while to remove their track suits. I ran my leg, arrived exhausted, and was promptly asked to run it again, and again.

S.K.: Freddie? Stanley. Can you talk?

F.R.: Sure.

S.K.: OK, the scene in the morgue. I think you're nearly there, but ... maybe it's a little too long, too complicated ...

F.R.: It's pretty well the way Arthur wrote it.

S.K.: Do you know where the Manhattan morgue is situated?

F.R.: No, I don't.

S.K.: I think I better find out. It might help.

F.R.: Stanley, more or less the whole sequence is an interior. I mean, find out by all means, but ...

S.K.: I have this doctor in New York I can call.

F.R.: Fine. I doubt if it'll make a lot of difference knowing the address, but ...

S.K.: Might be worth it.

The next day he called back to tell me that the morgue was situated on 30th Street and, I think he said, Third Avenue. I did not find that this knowledge much affected the emendations to the scene. However, it lent the stage directions an authenticity which seemed to convince Stanley. I was licensed to go on to the next scene. He always knew what he didn't want; never what he did. Whenever I sent him a new bunch of pages he would leave me without a reaction for an indeterminate period, while he considered them. In my first euphoria, I imagined that I had some almost instinctive notion of what he liked. That confidence was eroded as the weeks passed. Even after I had read it through, I was quite unable to guess what he would applaud and what he would ask me to do again. Sometimes he would leave me in doubt for several days. As the days and weeks went by, I wrote and I waited and I wrote again. Was it a deliberate policy to reduce me from independence to the service of his desires? I doubt if it required any such conscious scheme for him to behave as capriciously he did: it is natural for directors, of whatever skill, to seek to turn writers into their creatures. The frog and the scorpion can never contract out of their allotted roles.

S.K.: Freddie? *Ici* Kubrick. How goes it?

F.R.: *Seega, seega*, as the Greeks say.

S.K.: They do? What do they mean by that?

F.R.: Slowly, but steadily.

S.K.: What do you think Bill makes a year as a doctor in New York?

F.R.: You asked me that before.

S.K.: Think he makes as much as two hundred grand?

F.R.: With the kind of practice Bill has, yes, I do.

S.K.: Can you find out?

F.R.: How about calling your doctor friend? The one that gave you the address of the morgue. He'd know.

S.K.: (After a pause) I don't talk to him any more.

F.R.: You quarrelled with him?

S.K.: We don't talk any more. Don't ask your agent. Don't you know anybody else in New York?

F.R.: There's always Stanley Donen.

S.K.: How is he?

F.R.: I think he's OK. Wishes he was directing a movie. Why don't you call him? I know he'd like to hear from you.

S.K.: I like Stanley.

F.R.: Call him.

S.K.: I haven't spoken to him for so long. You think as much as two hundred grand? Sounds about right to me. Don't make that apartment too big, OK? Oh, and listen, would you take another look at the dream scene? I'm not sure the dream isn't a little too wordy, too literary the way Arthur has it.

F.R.: I did say that.

S.K.: Would you look at it again? See if you can come up with something more ... sexy and ... contemporary maybe.

Trying to substitute one dream for another is a trying exercise. How can you be sure that there isn't a better one? I built a sequence on an occasion when Sylvia and I were on holiday in Martinique. One afternoon I had a fever and stayed in bed while she went to the beach. The couple in the next room, whom I had never seen, came in and began to have sex. I could only *just*, yet very clearly, hear what they said and guess what they were doing. The man was being quite violent with the woman, but when she cried out, it was with pleasure. Imagining a beautiful, young woman and a passionate, implacable lover, I lay alone and listened, without shame (since without choice), to the rhythmic gasps which preceded the end of their performance. Quite soon after that, the couple left their room. I could not resist going to the window in order to catch a sight of them on the way to the beach. When they came out of the building, they were a middle-aged couple, neither comely nor unusual. The man was careful to help his wife along the unevenly set stones of the pathway. I wished my experience on Alice and had her dream of a kind of liquid wall between her and the glamorous couple next door.

Towards the end of March 1995, I again reached the last scene and told myself that I had yet again finished the first draft of Stanley's still untitled movie. I now intended to make it clear that it was time that I was paid. Virginia Woolf scorned Somerset Maugham because 'he has to write for money', but that is how, if not why, some of us make our living.

Following my usual routine, I sent the script to the William Morris office in London, asking Jane Annakin (who was now back after her surgery) to have copies made and sent to Stanley, to me and to Ron Mardigian, in California. In that way, Ron would have undeniable evidence that a payment was due. As Woody Allen once said, show-business is indeed a business; otherwise it would be called show-show.

Having confirmed that the script had reached London, Sylvia and I went for ten days to Venice, Asolo (where Robert Browning stayed soon after his elopement with Elizabeth Barrett) and Trieste, a city which I had wanted to visit ever since Jo Janni gave me the complete works of Italo Svevo, the pseudonym of a businessman called Ettore Schmitz. Schmitz and Schnitzler are not far apart phonetically, nor had they been very distant from each other in space and time. They were born within a year of each other and lived under the wide imperial mantle of Franz Josef II, whose longevity gave his monarchy the illusion of permanence.

Trieste was once the *entrepôt* to Vienna. It was a thriving – if reluctant – part of the Austro-Hungarian empire until the city was attached to Italy by the Treaty of Versailles. It was also an ideal place in which to try to forget that Stanley was reading my script. By staying away from contact for two weeks, I was surely allowing him ample time to think, and think again.

Trieste is a bourgeois and commercial city. Its canal lacks Venetian charm; the new Serbian Orthodox cathedral, with its pungent incense and iconostasis, is the only sign of Byzantine influence. The city seems as solid and as inimical to the imagination as its mercantile citizens. Unlike those in Vienna and in Germany, its synagogue (perhaps the largest and least charming in Europe) survived the war and stands, a grey fortress of respectability, not far from the Stock Exchange where Ettore Schmitz's fellow-citizens – and fictional characters – came and went. Svevo himself was a secular Jew, who married into a Gentile family of paint manufacturers. Lacking the authority which medicine gave Schnitzler, Svevo had a wry, self-deprecating manner, but he observed human foibles, not least his own, with something of Schnitzler's sadly accurate worldliness.

In order to widen his business contacts, Svevo decided to improve his English. His teacher was an Irish exile, temporarily resident in Trieste, whose name was James Joyce. In this way he became at least part of the inspiration for James Joyce's Bloom (his wife too was immortalized, as Anna Livia Plurabelle). Discovering that his teacher was a novelist, the shy Svevo asked Joyce to read something he himself had written. Expecting the embarrassing effusions of an amateur, Joyce was amazed by his employer's innovative assurance.

When Joyce became famous, he praised Svevo's work to literary circles in Paris. Thanks to his advocacy, Svevo's third novel, *The Confessions of Zeno* – one of the first books to follow the form of a psychoanalytic 'cure' – made him famous. Its anti-hero is *un homme moyen sensuel* trying desperately to give up smoking; he is perpetually having his last cigarette. On Joyce's invitation, Svevo went to Paris to talk about his work. On his way home, his chauffeur had an accident, not far from Trieste. Fatally injured, Svevo was laid by the side of the road to await the ambulance. While he was lying there, someone asked him if there was anything he wanted.

'Do you happen to have a cigarette?'

'I am afraid not.'

'Pity,' said Svevo, 'that really would have been a last cigarette.' He died not long afterwards.

Richard Burton (the Arabist not the actor) was British consul in Trieste for many years. The Earl of Derby had heard that the post was free and that, in the days when the pound was sovereign, it carried a salary of six hundred a year, though no duties attached to it. 'I thought of you at once,' Derby told his protégé. Producers sometimes say the same thing to flatter screenwriters, but there are always duties.

We enjoyed the grand unpretentiousness of Trieste enough almost to forget about Stanley Kubrick. However, I did happen to buy Claudio Magris's *Il mito Absburgico nella letteratura Austriaca moderna* and found myself reading about Arthur Schnitzler. I could not help wondering whether Kubrick would invite me to continue to a second draft and how much work it would entail. My desire for a favourable response owed more to my hatred of losing than to any sense that I was doing genuinely creative work. Even as I hoped to be summoned yet again to bondage, I dreamed of resuming the autonomy of the novelist. However, I had also promised my son Paul that, when I was free, I would write a script of *The Thought Gang*. Would Herakles have been happy without his labours?

The first thing I saw in the stack of post which awaited us was a fat copy of the script from the William Morris office in London. To my alarm and amazement, it was jacketed in a blue folder with the brazen WM logo on it. Underneath it was an envelope with a St Albans postmark. Inside was a single yellow sheet. As I read it, I felt sick, and angry.

I handed it to Sylvia. 'He hasn't even read it,' I said. 'Two weeks and he hasn't even fucking *read* it.'

Sylvia said, 'Are they mad or what, your agents?'

'Mad *and* what. How could they do that? How could they?'

Kubrick's note told us that he was too upset ('I could scarcely believe my eyes,' he wrote) at finding the script in a William Morris folder to be able to read it. He had put it aside rather than read it in a 'negative frame of mind'. He asked, with coldly itemized precision, that I discover who, apart from Mardigian, had read the script, how many copies were made and who, 'in London, NY and LA', received them?

After ten days of what now proved to have been vacuous suspense, I was so dismayed and disappointed that I could hardly understand what S.K. had to be upset about. I knew that he made a fetish of secrecy, but I hardly appreciated the intensity of his hermetic obsession. I was furious at the ineptitude of whatever idiot had bound the script in William Morris's colours, but my immediate response to Stanley was (when I look back) surprisingly unrepentant:

Dear Stanley,
We have just walked in the door, after a few days in Italy, and found your 'letter'. Great homecoming. Let me set the record straight: it is my habit, when a script is finished, to send a copy to my agents in London for forwarding to LA ... Alas, I forgot about those bloody awful folders ... I told (Jane's) assistant that no one but you was to have a copy, with the

exception of Mardigian ... He is a man of honour, a close friend and ... responsible for my business life. I cannot accept that I can be forbidden to file a text with an intimate friend and adviser as evidence of what I have done as the result of his deal-making. It would be ... alien to Ron's character and discreet nature to show a script in development to anyone. So: *the script has not been shown to anyone else and copies of it do not exist except in the cases I have said*: you have one, I now have two ... and one is on file in California with an agent (on whom) I have relied for twenty years.

We all have our foibles and yours, in the present case, are both understandable and paramount ... I might have hoped that the seriousness with which I have approached this work ... might dispense me from accusations of treachery or bad faith...

These last days, I have waited in rather pathetic hope of your endorsement of the new work on the script. Instead, I find that I have committed a 'crime' as inadvertent as that well-intentioned steadying of the Ark of the Covenant which led to G-d striking Uzzah dead. I always felt sorry for Uzzah, and now find I *am* Uzzah. If I had sent you my only copy, and risked losing the whole thing, I might now be smiling. But I am not...

On re-reading, this letter does not strike an appropriate note. It is at once too defiant and too sorry for itself. However, that is what I wrote. Although I did not read it in that light at the time, Stanley's instant response was remarkably patient and friendly. He denied, quite rightly, that he had ever accused me of treachery. His dread that the source and nature of the project would become known in California was, I now realize, well-founded (though it did not happen). I might assure him jokingly, as I did, that there was no risk of anyone in the

William Morris office having read the script, since I had never had any indication that any of them could read, but I had underestimated the curiosity which anything to do with Kubrick was likely to excite. He was afraid that I had 'compromised his deal-making and casting efforts on the film'. I was both chastened and furtively delighted to learn that he proposed to make them.

Furthermore, he told me, 'even if you don't understand why this is so', he thought that his credentials *as a producer* entitled him to more than having his concerns being offhandedly dismissed as one of his 'foibles'. He continued to reproach me, in what now appear quite mild terms, for sending the screenplay to California without his knowledge or approval and even before he had seen it. No writer he had ever worked with had ever done any of those things. 'Freddie,' he began again, 'this is far from being a foible.' If he had known what I intended to do he would not have started working with me. Nevertheless, he was quite ready to 'put all this behind us if ...' There followed a trio of conditions, binding me to secrecy henceforth. The fax was signed 'Regards', unlike those that preceded William Morris's stupidity, which always ended 'Best regards'.

Since I had never in the least intended to breach the dome of silence which he had lowered over the project, it was more a relief than a humiliation to go along with Stanley's demands. If I made haste to apologize, I did not wholly renounce my right to act in my own interests. The fact that Stanley had referred to himself as a 'producer' prompted me to add a rider to my assurances:

R.M. may bear the odious title of 'agent' but he has never broken faith with me ... I wish I could say as much of producers, executives and directors (I have been swindled out of credit and money). When I sent Ron the script, it was as evidence of having performed contractual obligations. Such things are no part of what interests me in my dealings with you, but life has taught both of us lessons, not always the same ones, and it is hard to forget them . . .

The best sentence, for me, in your letter, is 'I am quite ready to put this behind us'. I'm for that, as you can well imagine.

Stanley's response was that he wanted to see all the copies which had been made and to be sure that none lingered in the Morris office files. He went on to ask me to tell him what computer I used so that he might instruct me on how to make back-up disks ('which you should do anyway because hard drives can crash and loose [*sic*] all your data'). He went on to promise that he would read the new pages and go over the whole thing carefully. 'I suppose we should think about talking later in the week . . .' The happiest omen in the letter was at the end. It was once again signed 'Best regards'.

I should indeed have acquired the habit he recommended and made regular copies of everything. However, I am industrious without being efficient; the hard drive on my PC did indeed crash some two years later and I lost many files that I should be glad still to have. Stanley's own expertise in the field of electronics was, of course, legendary; his house was full of the latest equipment. During the course of our later labours, he asked me to send him a disk of the script so far, in order that he could play around with it himself. I did as he asked and was surprised when, some time later, he suggested that I fax him some pages with certain minor alterations on them.

I said, 'Why don't you save time and put them in yourself on the computer? You got the disk I sent you, didn't you?'

'Yes, I did, but . . . OK, I lost it.'

Four days later another letter arrived, by hand. It began: 'This is the first time that I have worked with anyone at such a distance and in such a remote, producer-like fashion, and taking all that into account I think the first draft screenplay is pretty amazing, with some absolutely wonderful things in it . . .' It went on to say that the second draft would definitely prove to be more than just a wash and a rinse and it might be necessary to work in a slightly different way. His usual way with other writers was that once a structure was agreed, each scene would be written, with a lot of discussion before and after, and without moving on until it was right. He acknowledged that this was not exactly 'a writer's dream' but that that was what it was going to take. If we were to go on, he would make detailed notes and we could get together and discuss them. That, he said, ought to give me a pretty good idea of what there might be left to do. The contract, he reminded me, gave him four weeks during which to exercise his first call on my services, but he didn't think it would take anything like that long to do the notes and have the discussion. However, if I decided against working as he proposed, he wouldn't make the call. He would, of course, tell Warner Brothers that I had completed the first draft and tell them to pay whatever was owed at that stage.

Despite his warm tone, he was still worried about Mardigian's copy of the script, which had not reached him yet from LA, but that did not prevent him from appending 'Best regards'. My joy at his remarks was, of course, redoubled by the *rapprochement* which they promised. He never referred to the incident again, although Mardigian was, from that time on, always referred to as 'the trusted Ron'.

I did not relish the idea of making daily, or even weekly, trips to St Albans in order to thrash out scenes face to face, but I announced my willingness to do so. In the event, Stanley was no keener than I to sacrifice his privacy. We continued to talk frequently, but at a distance.

May 1995. Notebook entry: 'We agreed to be in regular, even daily, touch by fax/phone. Spared the rack, I remounted the treadmill. I have been on it now for something like four weeks. As with the first draft, things began well. S.K. had decided, and asked me to accept as a condition of continuing, that the forty-two pages which he had admired so unconditionally before Christmas were now regrettably not of a piece with A.S.'s tale and had to be reconsidered, if not junked (they were *almost* junked).'

Stanley conceded that his revised opinion of the opening sequences might come to me, as it had to him, as an 'appalling surprise'. He insisted that the quality of the work was not in question, only its unbalancing effect on what followed. I saw the force of his argument and neither resented nor challenged it. Reason can have its place, even with intellectuals.

S.K.: This has got nothing to do with not *liking* the stuff you did before, it's just that maybe it was, OK, too good. I mean, we don't want the thing to start off so well we can't keep it up. If Alice is as sexually, OK, forward as you made her, then she has no place to go later.

F.R.: Gotcha.

S.K.: Maybe the whole section is kinda *too* good. Maybe we can't keep things at that level. Maybe it just shouldn't *be* that good.

F.R.: You're not seriously suggesting we should deliberately make it *worse*?

S.K.: I don't know.

F.R.: Stanley, I take the point about Alice. What worries me isn't changing it, but the idea that making the whole sequence somehow *worse* is going to make things better later on – frankly that's mad. What we have to do is start well and get better.

S.K.: If we can.

F.R.: We have to believe we can.

S.K.: So listen, will you do it over? I mean, reduce it and make her . . .

F.R.: I said I would. I will. I'll try and fax you something at the end of the day.

S.K.: Talk to you tomorrow.

Stanley had been more tactful than usual – almost apologetic – when he sprang his 'appalling surprise'. He probably feared that I might use his earlier enthusiasm to confute him. He had been at pains to break the bad news gently and I accepted the force of his argument. He soon resumed his habitual *attentisme*: without specific ideas of his own, he was reluctant to approve mine. Did his attitude of chiding passivity derive from his experience as a still photographer? There is nothing that a serious photographer wants less than a model who smiles. On the contrary, he waits for his subjects to be bled of personality. He clicks on, and on, until they reveal their real appearance by no longer having the energy or the will to put a good face on themselves.

Stanley liked to amuse, and – sometimes – to be amused, but he did not want the script to be dressed up with wisecracks.

He waited until a kind of exhaustion delivered scenes which were much bonier than I might care to write for myself. As with actors (and particularly actresses), he cared less about what other people felt than about how they catered to his needs. I feel that the still – or *almost* still – image was fundamental to Kubrick's vision of cinema. The density and care with which the frame was so often composed in his work owed very little to any appetite for motion. Some of the most memorable moments in *Barry Lyndon*, for instance, were all but motionless: the highwayman and his assistant looking at Barry outside the wayside inn; Barry with the two whores – a scene artfully derivative from Hogarth; Marisa Berenson on the terrace when Barry declares his love for her. To find *Barry Lyndon* boring is to admit to having no eye.

Only so much of a work of art can be foreseen. As Stanley confessed to me, nothing in the story-board of *Barry Lyndon*, still less in the sketch characterization of the smaller roles, envisaged the brilliant invention of Leonard Rossiter as Captain Quin. Not the least of Kubrick's unrecognized skills was that of allowing space for the genius of others to flourish. If he had no patience with mediocrity, he could be accommodatingly deferential when it came to talent he admired. Rossiter, he conceded, had made something unforgettable out of a cardboard character. Actors might be abused, or worked to exhaustion, but Kubrick never regarded them, as Hitchcock was said to, as 'cattle'.

The director can control images most tellingly when they tend towards the static. Vigilance determined Stanley's world: he read contracts, and measured advertisements, with the same meticulousness that he reshot or recut scenes. Like a still photographer, he always hoped that something better might come of repetition. He was a huntsman who watched, and waited, but could never say for what exactly. He asked me to rewrite scenes, without any specific indication of what was wanted, less out of sadism than because he had all the time in the world to look forward to something better. I never knew anyone in the movies less distressed by the protraction of the process. He might be aware of what other directors were doing, and of how prolific they were, but he showed no envy and no inclination to catch up with them. He played his chess without a clock. Jews are sometimes alleged to live outside the world of hope in which Christians rejoice: Judaism has laws, but no timetable for salvation.

May 1995. Notebook entry: 'S.K. has a tendency to jeer, while seeming to be personally "intuitive". I am not always amused by regular references to B. Streisand and to my supposed facility with American dialogue. He is not *nasty* but a little sarcastic ... I have never been good at tactics in relations with other people; as my bad losing proves, I am woefully sincere. I always tend to think that if I am candid and passionate, all will be well. These last couple of weeks, however, I have had recourse to calculation. When S.K. is unresponsive, I go silent on the telephone; I cease to send amiable notes with my pages; I work to rule. Let's see how you like it, buster.'

S.K.: Freddie?

F.R.: Oh hello, Stanley.

S.K.: You OK?

F.R.: I'm fine.

S.K.: Yeah? You really sound it. I got the pages. Freddie?

F.R.: I'm listening.

S.K.: This a bad time?

F.R.: No.

My cold tone prompted him to become charming again. We began to make quicker progress. I feared that writing this movie, which still had no title, would last longer than the Trojan War, but the stack of approved scenes grew more quickly. Concerned that we still had no title, I faxed a suggestion: THE FEMALE SUBJECT. He did not acknowledge receipt. Some days later he proposed EYES WIDE SHUT. I refrained from any response except that of refraining from response. It was his movie.

12.5.95. Notebook entry: 'One of his entourage refers to him as "the in-house deity"; he cannot be wrong and he cannot be contradicted. He has no interest in "psychology" (which is fine) nor does he want to acknowledge the form of a film as a matter of deliberate structure, which is less fine. Although he respects "Arthur" enough to make him unassailable, he does so more to block improvements, on my part, than out of any articulate critical sense; it is convenient to impose fidelity. As a *quondam* chess player, one might have expected a Nabokovian respect for the game of art as an unfolding pattern of strategies, but S.K. is enough of a regular American to dread any open admission of being an artist or having a theory. He has rareness, but he needs to remain commonplace, even vulgar, for fear of being the new Orson. He is so unlike Welles that he refrains from all public parade of his fame; he refuses interviews and scarcely goes out at all. (When A.F. calls to give me a message, he sometimes *says* that S.K. has had to go out, but this is a convention, I suspect, like saying that madame is not at home.)

'S.K. is grudging with praise and never likes *part* of a scene; either he accepts the whole thing or, except for tiny points, rejects it all. He is shy rather than loud in saying "no", but he *never* asks what I meant or solicits a performance or elucidation. While he is a *producer*, I am (perhaps) indispensable; when he becomes a director, how long will I survive?'

S.K.: Been watching the trial?

F.R.: Quite a bit, yes.

S.K.: See that guy giving evidence, what was his name? Shipp, that his name? Used to hang out at O.J.'s place, Rockingham, see him on the stand?

F.R.: Yes, I did.

S.K.: What did you think?

F.R.: Kinda sad. He really thought he mattered to O.J. and ... I doubt he did.

S.K.: The way he said 'I'm sorry, O.J.', you see that?

F.R.: Understandable.

S.K.: Think so? Said he's been 'a willing slave'? Guy's a toady, don't you think so?

F.R.: O.J. was his god. Think he did it?

S.K.: Doesn't everybody? Everybody thinks what nobody says.

F.R.: We're back to anti-Semitism again.

S.K.: Thought any more about the orgy?

F.R.: Some.

S.K.: How about the Romans? Didn't they have a lot of orgies?

F.R.: I thought that was de Mille.

S.K.: There has to be some descriptions of Roman orgies some-place. Can you check?

F.R.: You're not actually intending to show people having sex, are you?

S.K.: I don't know. I wish I did. See what you can come up with. Let your imagination go.

We were working on, scene by scene, towards an area where I was convinced that we had to have a climax that would knit the movie into a sustained narrative. I admired Schnitzler, but not as unconditionally as S.K. found convenient. The closer we got to the orgy, and what followed, the less fruitful it was going to be to proceed only step by step.

If the thing was to have an overall shape, its end had to have something to do with its beginning. *Full Metal Jacket* had relied on the twist of the female sniper and her killing. Killing another woman would not be enough for (the title seemed to have been settled now) *Eyes Wide Shut*. Day after day, Stanley mocked my obsession with things having a shape. I did not know how we would ever finish the script until we agreed its form. My desire to do what was right and necessary was seconded by my longing to dismount from the treadmill on which I had embarked. 'For gold, for praise, for glory'? Who knew?

May 1995. Notebook entry: 'He is morbidly afraid of giving away any of his secrets, the best of which may be that he has none. His technique is very technical; he was an early addict

135

of computers and the whole machinery of computerization chimes with his desire to consider all the possibilities of a situation. What cannot, however, be analysed into a series of choices is originality itself, which remains the ragamuffin property of the urchin talent. It is for this "reason" that I am both desirable (since I supply dialogue about which he is regularly flattering) and *menacing*, since my ideas just might shatter the notion that a work of art can be manufactured out of finite, manipulable elements. I anger S.K., in an impersonal sort of way, when I remind him that the possible readings and versions of any anecdote, however apparently "perfect", are legion, if not infinite. The fear that a story can get away from him – a man who takes endless precautions against anything unforeseen – lies behind all his caution. He does not want anything to escape him. This desire makes him the prisoner of what he dreads without disarming the dreadful. The recluse imagines that if he can reduce the possibility of surprises the world will become orderly, but the more order he contrives, the more it is vulnerable to fortune. The wish to eliminate chance leads to the madness of which method is the symptom. By the scrupulousness of his inspections, the care with which he makes sure that the casual never falls on his head, S.K. becomes a Damocles without a sword, a man threatened by a thread.

'He avoids contact but he cannot control his curiosity; he has impersonal knowledge of the price of whores everywhere. The worldliness of the recluse is a function of his dread of missing the very things which he has excluded from his life. S.K.'s obsession with "security" renders him utterly insecure and means that he is always under surveillance. When I am told that he had "slipped out", the phrase marvellously captures his unconfessed yearning to escape from the very regime which he has decreed for himself. In creative terms, he has done something similar: in order not to be contaminated by extraneous, uncontrollable contributions, he makes himself inaccessible to any ideas which might clash with his own.

'The tyrant is a man so threatened by apprehensions of being overthrown that he must reduce everyone else to impotence. In the process of not being deceived or misled, he repudiates all advice and regards anything that he would prefer not to hear as disinformation. Prey to rumour, he is unavailable to the truth. The comedy of S.K. is that of a man so hermetically preserved against unwanted contact that he has to "slip out" in order to have any unexpected experience at all. His curiosity, even in the realm of routine intelligence, is limited by his isolation and thus excited by it.

'The self-anaesthetist suffers the same torments as the self-torturer, but he does not have the cruel satisfaction of feeling anything. He is at once aloof and tentatively crude, as if seeking to escape his own reputation. He told me that the producer M.N., when married to a notoriously "difficult" star, once said to a director with whom she was being impossible that all it needed to restore her to equilibrium was "a little head".'

S.K.: Freddie? Stanley. Can you talk?

F.R.: Sure.

S.K.: You watching the tennis?

F.R.: Not while I'm working.

S.K.: Listen, ah, the script, there seems to be a lot of, you know, chunks of stuff, stage directions, that I find difficult to read. Goes right across the page in big fat paragraphs.

F.R.: You asked me to tell you everything I could think of that might be relevant. I can stop.

S.K.: I find that right across the page stuff hard to read.

F.R.: Believe me, it's not something I do for my own pleasure.

S.K.: You know what? I kinda wish in scripts people wrote the *dialogue* right across the page, like they do in plays, and made the stage directions like, you know, narrow and centred like you do the speeches.

F.R.: That could probably be done. It'd break the habits of a lifetime, but...

S.K.: If you'd at least kinda break up those big chunks of yours.

F.R.: OK.

S.K.: Anything on Roman orgies yet?

F.R.: I'll fax you. Didn't you have an orgy in *Spartacus*?

S.K.: See what you can find. Did you read a novel called *A Soldier of the Great War* yet?

F.R.: I've heard of it, haven't read it, why?

S.K.: I'd like to know what you think. I'll send it to you.

F.R.: You already did the Great War, didn't you?

S.K.: Long time ago.

F.R.: Believe me, you did. I never saw more believable battle scenes, except on newsreels. Where did you do that?

S.K.: Germany.

F.R.: *Germany*?

S.K.: Sure. They wouldn't let us do them in France. Germany was cheaper then.

F.R.: Where did you get all the soldiers from?

S.K.: I had this German production manager, he organized it so we had these special police units, you know? The Germans didn't have an official army in those days, but ... They had these ... He organized it. Found the battlefield too. He had an incredible eye. We went out one day looking for locations in the snow. He suddenly stopped the car and went out into the fields, near Dachau I think it was, and found just what we needed. That dip in the ground and the hill beyond it. He had some eye.

F.R.: How long did it take to shoot?

S.K.: It took a lot of organizing.

F.R.: I'll bet. How many cameras?

S.K.: Maybe six. It was pretty complicated.

F.R.: How many times did you have to do it?

S.K.: I forget. More than once though. First time, we had everything set up, all the cameras that were going to pick up the advance as it went forward. I gave them the signal and they came out of the trenches, advanced right across no-man's-land and, before I could do anything about it, they went right on and captured the, you know...

F.R.: Ant-hill.

S.K.: Couldn't stop them. So I had them come all the way back and I said to this guy that he had to explain to them, because I didn't speak any German, that they were supposed to be French infantrymen, OK?, and they were *not* supposed to go right on up the goddam hill and capture the ... you know. They had to go slow enough for the cameras to pick them up and finally, well, they had to slow down and pretty well stop and then...

F.R.: They had to fall back, right?

S.K.: ...fall back. So I asked him to explain this to these special police units. He went over and started to tell them and suddenly I could hear them all laughing.

F.R.: *Laughing*?

S.K.: I asked him what was funny and he told me: he'd just explained to them that they were supposed to advance like French soldiers. So that's what they did the next time, they came out kinda slow and ... that was how we got to shoot the scene. I'll tell you something: battlefields are no fun to shoot in.

F.R.: Did you really do all the Vietnam stuff in England?

S.K.: Sure. Why not? Problem we had there was different.

F.R.: What was that?

S.K.: Problem there wasn't while we were shooting. That was fine. We could keep everybody out of the way, no problem. Problem was at night, when there was nobody there. We had to leave it like it was, this big piece of waste land. And what happened was, local kids came in and vandalized the battlefield. We'd come back in the morning and they'd vandalized the battlefield.

F.R.: So what did you do?

S.K.: Fenced it. We fenced the whole damn thing. I'll send you the Helprin book. When'll I get something on orgies?

16.5.95.

Dear Stanley,

Suetonius gossips only about the sexual activities of the emperors whom he wishes to mock or disparage. He does not describe what they do, except very briefly. It is alleged that Tiberius liked to be sucked off by small children, male I think, in his Capri swimming pool. Nero fucked his mother and then, so they say, had her killed in a collapsible boat. Caligula did many things of a politically incorrect nature, but we cannot admire him wholeheartedly on that account. Claudius's wife, Messalina, as Robert Graves reminded us, prostituted herself in the common brothels because the imperial yard did not measure up.

The Roman 'orgy' is something of a Hollywood fantasy, since rich Romans could always do as they pleased, sexually, with their slaves and hence needed no playboy to license or arrange their pleasures. Arranged pleasures tended to be gastronomic, and disgusting. The best 'accounts' of Roman sexual activity are visual (e.g. Pompeian wall paintings, especially the brothel in which various positions were illustrated above the cubicles, rather in the style of those cafés on the Costa Brava with illustrated menus for pigs who can point but not read). Petronius's 'orgy' in the *Satyricon* is, I think, described only because it is a jumped-up slave who is its host and hence it is more a social sneer than an erotic blueprint (compare the Jewish joke about the synagogue janitor who overheard the rabbi's sermon to his rich congregants in which he reminded them that, whatever their pretentions, 'We're all nothing'; the janitor called out from the back of the hall, 'You'se right, rabbi, I'm *nothing*!' To which the rabbi said, pointing at him, 'Look who wants to be nothing!').

Rich Romans did as they pleased all the time. Cicero pointed a scandalized finger at Clodia, in the *Pro Milone*, but only for courtroom purposes and because he was a middle-class upstart without the confidence, virility or access required to gain entry to the best women . . .

I suggested that the orgy take the form of a sort of sexual mall, perhaps in the library of the big house. I had in mind a large room rather like the old library of St John's College, Cambridge, in which there were 'bays' with tables for study. I also returned to the matter of the plot. It was, I argued, seriously unsatisfactory unless, for instance, the man I had called Ziegler was somehow involved both in the orgy and in Bill's escape from danger. To avoid resolving the issue, merely because Schnitzler had left it all in the air, would be to make the same mistake as Antonioni when he failed, at the end of *Blow Up*, to let us have any idea why anyone had been murdered, or by whom.

S.K.: Freddie? Can you talk?

F.R.: What's happening?

S.K.: Listen, you like things to have a shape, don't you?

F.R.: I believe I said so. Yes, I do. It shows you're not . . . bluffing.

S.K.: Does it?

F.R.: I think so. So does Aristotle. You don't.

S.K.: Tell you what, suppose you try it your way. Make Ziegler the man at the party and . . you know what, don't you? We're going to need a whole new scene, at the end of the picture, before Bill goes home the last time, where he confronts Ziegler about the Baroness, or whatever she is now, and Ziegler tells him the whole story and . . . if that's what you want him to do.

F.R.: I certainly do. And I always did. I think he should go to his house, somehow knowing that . . . Or better, Bill gets called up maybe to go and see Ziegler and . . .

S.K.: You like things to have a shape. Give it a shape. Then we'll see. Freddie . . .

F.R.: Yeah?

S.K.: Can you give me some idea who those people are at the orgy, some kind of background, so I can kinda believe in what they're doing?

Not long afterwards, I faxed Stanley a document which purported to be an extract from a highly classified FBI report on an association which had begun among certain admirers of the late President Kennedy. These people were said mostly to be rich and hostile to the line taken by the Democratic party once it had been captured by 'hicks'. The fraternity admired JFK's impudent defiance of public morality, while appearing to conform to it, and adhered to a group whose habits were outwardly conformist and who, at the same time, practised among themselves a completely hedonistic way of life. Their slogan was 'Enough is never enough'. They called themselves 'The Free'.

The main expression of this freedom was sexual: members were recruited only among friends of the friends and their induction involved an undertaking to seek pleasure for themselves and not to deny it to others of the fraternity. Men began the club and, during the early period, sometimes hired women to participate in their pleasures, which were always taken on private premises. No journalist was ever admitted to the group, although owners of newspapers (who could make sure that nothing was ever printed about it) were certainly included.

The decision not to continue using hookers was taken by the club's so-called 'Senate' after a scandal in which a prostitute broke the code and sold an interview to a local TV station, luckily in Arkansas where she and it could be 'taken care of'. It was, I said, recognised in the 1980s that prostitution had become part of the entertainment business and, for that reason, that whores could no longer be relied upon to be discreet.

The consequence was that women began to be admitted as full members. This coincided 'luckily' with the 'women's movement', which had seemed to threaten the phallocratic ethos of the Free; in fact, it liberated a generation of women who shared their ideas. Recruitment of 'free' women was never a problem and encouraged a hermetic society of wealthy/successful people whose sophistication gave them a wide appetite for secret pleasures.

The Free were neither a sect nor a cult. The responsibility for dealing with leaks (to the press or local police) was vested in 'The Plumbers', who sealed off all escapes of information and who, in cases of potential embarrassment, moved smartly and with sufficient funds to limit the danger. The rule was *never* to speak of The Free among Slaves (those who observed conventional morality out of fear or convention). 'Freedom' depended on exclusivity and absolute loyalty. Vigilant screening of new members was important, but novelty was essential to revive appetite.

Four Freedoms were sacred: Freedom from Democracy, from Correctness, from Publicity and from Love.

I went on to say that it was believed that The Plumbers, like Plato's Nocturnal Council, were a law unto themselves. There were rumours that transgressors had been dealt with summarily. No direct evidence, however, linked The Plumbers with the death of Frannie de Zoete (dead in a motel in Palm Beach) or Leslie van der Groot (drowned in a car belonging to a senator). The alertness of The Plumbers was occasionally tested by the Senate's covert introduction of a stranger into one of the (always masked) meetings. The ejection of the interloper was also a reminder to the membership of the need for secrecy. Often the intruder was a candidate for membership and the whole occasion something of a 'chilling charade'.

Husbands and wives were never recruited jointly and, if they wished to attend the same seminar, had to do so separately and, should they recognize each other, had to behave like strangers and never, of course, interfere in whatever the other was doing, no matter with whom. This had never caused a problem.

The Free had no known links with either religious or political extremisms, nor was membership limited to Democrats. The club was united in its indifference to public morality and charitable purpose. It was devoted to pleasure, and its pursuit. In that sense it was 'highly constitutional'. Snobbishness was prevalent; narrow-mindedness was not. The Free made every effort to remain immune to discovery, but that was part of its pleasure: the fear of exposure enhanced the joy of concealment. Life was a game, not a morality.

S.K.: Freddie?

F.R.: Hi, Stanley.

S.K.: Can you talk?

F.R.: Sure. Get the material I faxed you?

S.K.: That's the thing. Where'd you get this stuff?

F.R.: About The Free? Where do you think?

S.K.: This is Classified Material, how'd you get hold of it? I need you to tell me.

F.R.: You're kidding.

S.K.: I don't think so. Where'd you find this stuff? Did you hack into some FBI computer by chance or what?

F.R.: *Hack in*? Are you crazy? I can't hack into my own work without help. You asked me to give you some background on Ziegler and company. I gave it.

S.K.: Freddie, I need you to tell me totally honestly where you got this stuff. This is potentially...

F.R.: Stanley, totally honestly I got it where I get everything: out of my head.

S.K.: You telling me you made this up?

F.R.: But only because it's true. You asked for it, I did it. I enjoyed it as a matter of fact.

S.K.: It has no basis in fact?

F.R.: Stanley, I made it up, OK?

S.K.: How did you do that?

F.R.: Making things up's what I do for a living. It's pretty well *all* I do. I write fiction. I make things up. I look at the world and ... I make things up on the strength of what I see and hear, and guess. I do not mend fuses or water-ski or have a pension scheme. I made it up. It was fun; much more fun than . . .

S.K.: OK, as long as we're not . . . on potentially dangerous ground here. It's pretty convincing, you know that?

F.R.: Nice of you to say so. Think of it as an example of what I do when I'm free to play by myself. An apple for the teacher.

S.K.: And it didn't come from anywhere that might be . . . you know . . . embarrassing?

F.R.: Look, it came out of my head, fully-formed. How embarrassing is that? I made the whole damn thing up. It was not a big problem.

S.K.: How long did it take you?

F.R.: Maybe an hour, but I'm never going to tell you that.

S.K.: OK, so . . . will you go on to the next scene now?

Late May 1995. Notebook entry: 'Directors can never believe that there are people who find it easier to invent things than to steal them. It might damage their affectations of omnipotence. The tributes which Stanley pays to what I do in fields outside screenwriting are, I suspect, a substitute for admitting me to his confidence within the current project. Praise for, even deference to, my fiction is offered only to compensate for my exclusion from the creative heart of the movie. I have come to realize, painfully, that I am there to provide a script to which he can then apply himself without me. He is entirely uninterested in what *I* make of Schnitzler or might contribute apart from words on the page, a blueprint for performance and photography. He is not even prepared to listen to what I think, critically, of my own work. *He* thinks and then he makes his move. I make mine; he responds. All he requires of me is a text that can be made audible and visible.

'I used to think that what interested him was scandal. That is only partly so: what "amuses" him in scandal is the capacity of the camera to confront the unspeakable without blinking: its mechanical inability to distinguish between the human and the inhuman. The camera is free alike of scruples and of morals; by virtue of its cold nature, it flinches from nothing visible. Kubrick wishes he could be like that. Choosing what should be outrageous, he is grimly pleased to alarm, terrify or titillate an audience while himself remaining unexcited. He likes to be "clinical", as they say (his father was a doctor). Does he harp on the outrageous *because* he has willed himself to be immune to direct sensation and has to be stimulated by the shock he administers to his audience? The voyeuristic kick comes not from what he photographs but in observing (or even – through attendance figures – *counting*) the scandalized responses of others. My glib suspicion is that the only *serious* scandal for him is the Holocaust, which is why he will not, or cannot, deal with it.

'Could it be argued (if one bothered) that S.K.'s films "deal with" the collapse of routine safeguards against "unjust" violence, against unpunished cruelty? There is a tendency in them for innocence to be treated as a crime (this begins with *Paths of Glory*); trust only licenses disloyalty; innocuousness provokes harm. Any cure for evil is depicted, as in *A Clockwork Orange*, as itself an evil, if not the culmination of it (*très* Foucault!). In this way, "morals" – and hence God's supposed law – can be read as excuses for treating mundane evils as incurable. All human attempts to control the devil are conducive to greater cruelties and nastier devils.

'Does S.K. imagine himself to have been the victim of injustice? Unlike the usual moaners, he has avoided complaining about not receiving an Oscar. Does he care that the best director has never been Best Director? As cold comfort, he conducts his business with demanding vigilance. For the rest, he endures in strident silence and refrains from endearing shows of generosity. He is, however, a passionate lover of animals, especially his dogs, whose deaths he treats as bereavements. He confessed to feeling "not himself" after one of his pets died recently of lung cancer; he nursed the creature until the last minute and was painfully enumerative of its terminal symptoms.

'S.K. said to me, not long after Hitler's recent birthday, that A.H. had been "right about almost everything", a remark which, seen in the most genial available light, contains all the elements of outrageousness, challenge and horror which are largely to be found in his movies. Was he daring me to disagree, or to agree? What does it mean to mean, or not to mean, such a remark? I remember another Jewish boy at school who, during a football match, whispered in my ear, "Jew!" I suspect that S.K. was doing something similar. Among Jews, there is nothing some Jews will not say; the bully and the bullied have cruel affinities. I was, in a sense, forked: if I did not bridle, I was acquiescing in the fate which both S.K. and I might then "deserve"; if I dissented, it would prove that I couldn't lighten up. In the event, I was at once cowardly and disdainful; I treated the remark as an unamusing jest. With pitiless self-knowledge, Arthur Schnitzler once remarked "the eternal truth that no Jew has any real respect for his fellow Jew, ever". It would be pretty to believe that, with the establishment of the state of Israel (first mooted – after the failure of his writing career – by Schnitzler's friend Herzl), such mutual scorn is no longer necessarily the rule. I am not so sure.

'S.K. has said, more than once, 'What do we know about how Gentiles feel?" Yet he wants to suppress any overt allusion to Jewishness in our story. He takes joy in the surreptitious. Art and furtiveness are old associates (the jealous Daedalus "accidentally" murdered his talented nephew by pushing him over a cliff), and I have little doubt that, *le moment venu*, I could be subject to a similar shove. Jewishness is not something that unites us; on the contrary, it will license him to deal consciencelessly with me. Jews are often *real* Jews only with each other. Gentiles never suspect this. They accuse us of having a secret and common agenda: the only secret is that we practise on each other enmities, treacheries and ruthlessness which we might not dare to indulge in other directions. Do I exaggerate? We shall see.

'S.K. proceeds by indirection; who knows where, still less why? The anarchic charm of film is that "why" scarcely matters. Only fools and executives worry about motivation. The reason people do things can be explained, finally and fully, only by the entire history of the human race up until now. S.K.'s work could be viewed, schematically, as responding, in various ways, to the unspeakable (what lies beyond spoken explanation). How does this apply to *Barry Lyndon*? American critics such as Stephen Farber found an answer when they condemned the film as a declaration of secession from their world to Europe, S.K.'s evidence of emigration to another country. They saw him as a kind of artistic Benedict Arnold, ungratefully leaving their present for the antique world of European classics.

'There is a stubbornness in S.K. which requires him never to admit a mistake. For instance, he suddenly accused me of long-windedness, quite as if he himself had not solicited it, when he asked that the script read "more like a novel". He cannot confess that I was in any way *generous* in my prolixity.

He does not like those who do as he asks, the mark of the sado-masochist: what he can *say* that he wants is never quite what he does want. He seeks neither loyalty nor intimacy; both make betrayal more likely. Nothing embarrasses him more than sincerity. Life is about power, not sincerity. If I decide to become frigid, *then* he warms up. *Che noia!'*

I have quoted from my notebooks less in order to reveal my real feelings about Stanley than to remind myself of how exasperating he could be. It is rare for a writer to have recourse to his private confessional in order to say with what unambiguous fondness he regards other people. During the long weeks of working on *Eyes Wide Shut* (as it had now definitively become), I was both dedicated and dissident. Stanley was Eurystheus to my Herakles, the taskmaster for whom I was serving an unspecified lease of bondage. For gold? I was being paid, but not spoiled. For praise? Grudgingly offered and rarely for things that *I* was proud of. For glory? I still had little confidence that the movie would ever be made.

As well as bouts of chagrin at his failure to make me a genuine partner, I felt spasms of almost protective affection. Stanley was so determined to be aloof and unfeeling that my heart went out to him. Somewhere along the line he was still the kid in the playground who had been no one's first choice to play with. His early passion for photography licensed a kind of spying on the world which declared that he was not a happy part of it. Photography *demands* two-facedness; his hidden camera – concealing it in a shoebox had been one of Stanley's early ruses – gives the apparently innocent (and helpless) spectator an unsuspected third eye. The revenge of the secret (photographic) sharer is that he is a monster who can record surreptitiously what seems, on the face of things, to have left no trace.

Stanley's unique standing was, perhaps, more obvious to others than to himself. He had achieved autonomy by acute diplomacy no less than through cinematic genius. People imagined that he could do whatever he liked, but he knew more disappointments than others cared to count. He had nursed many projects which never, as they say, had legs. Before his Napoleon film was aborted, he had accumulated a library of some twenty thousand photographs of all the locations in which the Emperor had spent even one of his busy days. His intention had been to build the most important ones on the lot in England, but some other movies about Napoleon brought about his Waterloo.

F.R.: Haven't you ever wanted to make a Western?

S.K.: What do you mean?

F.R.: Do you admire Sergio Leone at all?

S.K.: Do you?

F.R.: Yes, I do, at times. Or do I admire Morricone? Both.

S.K.: I spent two years trying to do a Western, with Marlon.

F.R.: Which one was that?

S.K.: *One-Eyed Jacks*. Two years I spent on that.

F.R.: What happened?

S.K.: Marlon was going to star and produce.

F.R.: Did you not get along?

S.K.: I thought we did.

F.R.: What went wrong? Didn't you like him?

S.K.: Great actor. But he was also the producer. He couldn't make up his mind about things and he wouldn't let anybody else. We never got the story straight. We never got anything straight. You start these things and ... you never know when to stop. At the end of two years, Marlon decided to get decisive suddenly. He got everybody in and we had to sit round the table. He'd bought himself this stop-watch. He put this stop-watch on the table and he suddenly said that we had to make some decisions, get things going, so what he was going to do was he was going to allow everybody just three minutes to tell him what their problems were and that way we'd have an agenda and we could decide what needed to be done. He started round the table. I was sitting next to him, so I was going to be last, OK? The cameraman started in, then the location manager and then the casting director and each of them, as soon as he'd had three minutes, the buzzer would go and – bop! – that was all the time they got no matter if they'd finished or not. So, it went all the way round the table and Marlon looked at me and he said, 'Stanley, what're your problems?' And he pressed the button. 'You've got three minutes.' I said, 'Come on, Marlon, this is a stupid way to do things.' And he said, 'Now you've got two minutes fifty.' So I started with what I thought had to be done on page one and page two and I'd maybe got to page five when he said, 'That's it, you've had your three minutes.' So I said, 'Marlon, why don't you go fuck yourself?'

F.R.: I'll bet you did, and what did he say?

S.K.: He didn't. He just got up – we were in one of those bungalow things – he got up and walked into the bedroom and slammed the door. I said, 'What can he do? So he's walked out. He has to walk back sooner or later.' Someone said I shouldn'ta said what I said, but what else are you going to say when people act that way? He'd be back.

F.R.: And was he?

S.K.: No. He never came out of there. We sat around and finally we all went home. Maybe he wanted me out of there and he couldn't figure how else to do it. That was Marlon.

A film-maker, however grand, is always at the mercy of circumstances, unless he is the circumstance. Why would Stanley regard me as anything but a means to an end which had nothing to do with me? I *almost* sympathized with the patient impatience with which he had to wait for pages which – always assuming that he had hired the right hand – would allow him to be independent of any other creative intelligence. The better the director, the more frustrated he is bound to be by needing anyone else at all, even temporarily.

S.K.: That's a pretty good coupla scenes you sent me. You sure can do that stuff between husbands and wives.

F.R.: I do my best.

S.K.: I know that. Up to a certain point.

F.R.: Excuse me?

S.K.: Freddie, come on. Don't get me wrong. I know how hard you work. But you know something: I don't think a good writer can ever do his best work on a screenplay. Not for somebody else.

F.R.: What's this about?

S.K.: Are you watching the tennis?

F.R.: No, I'm working on this script.

S.K.: Freddie, come on … All I meant to say was, no writer who's really good is ever going to invest his full ego in work that some other guy is going to come in and direct. It's a psychological impossibility. It's not a question of how hard you work, there always has to be something you hold back.

F.R.: It's true. But I never said so.

S.K.: I was a writer, I'd be the same. Freddie, will you tell me something?

F.R.: Of course.

S.K.: Why don't you put the date on your pages?

F.R.: I usually date the faxes, don't I?

S.K.: I'd appreciate to have the date on every page.

F.R.: Who gives a shit about the date?

S.K.: You can get your computer to do it automatically.

F.R.: No. *You* can get my computer to do it automatically. I can't even get it to number the pages.

S.K.: Shift F8 and you've got the menu right in front of you. Put the date on the pages and I can refer back when I want to. Otherwise I can't tell which is which. Can you do that for me?

F.R.: I'll see what I can do.

S.K.: Go switch on the TV, OK? Agassi's murdering the guy.

Working for all those months with Stanley was like being in solitary confinement without the comfort of being alone. Our long conversations sometimes resembled those that Arthur Koestler's Rubashov conducted with the man in the next cell, in *Darkness at Noon*; at other times they were like his excruciating interviews with his inquisitors. I had the victimized honour of being the right-hand *apparatchik* of 'Chairman Stan', as I had heard him described. My duty, like Rubashov's, was to concede my complete submission to the needs of the Leader. At other times still, the initial K. reminded me also of Kafka. I might have been sentenced to serve time in the luxurious wing of his penal colony, alone with a personal computer that would print nothing but rewrites and a fax line which went through only to S.K.

I must not exaggerate: I continued to be exhilarated by working with the only director for whom I considered protracted peonage worth while. We continued to have long talks on many subjects apart from the film. Out of school, so to say, he solicited my views quite as if I were some venerable oracle. When I told him that I had been reading a foreign author, Claudio Magris for instance, he would ask apprehensively what language I was reading him in. Vanity was not his style; he never cited his own work with complacency and often admired other people's (what exactly he liked about a Spanish film called *The Red Squirrel* I was never able to understand). He could be pitiless, but never conceited. When I told him how brilliant I thought it was that he had allowed the passion between Ryan O'Neil and Marisa Berenson to develop in almost total silence and how immensely desirable it made her, he said, 'Did you hear the way she talked when she had to? The scene when she had to go to the village when the kid was going to have the accident?' He mocked the unalterably American cadences of her voice with enough jeering rage to suggest that he still resented the time he had wasted trying to get her to sound European.

'What else could I do with her but keep her quiet?'

'You made what she couldn't do work for you.'

'You have to work with what you've got, not what you wish you had.'

If we sometimes acted like buddies, there was between us an intimacy without commitment and, at times, heat without warmth. The screenwriter is cousin to Kafka's K. who, accused of crimes he has not committed and of treasons to a cause not his own, looks forward with prescient helplessness to being hounded to oblivion 'like a dog'.

31.5.95. Notebook entry: 'I have now sent him up to page ninety (out of a putative 125–130). I can at least imagine that school will soon be out. What is less certain is whether there will be another term and whether I shall still be in the top class. If he agrees that I have now pretty well cracked the orgy, the holidays cannot be far away, though I would be unwise to count the days.

'I have never met anyone for whom I had less consistent feelings. I think I admire him still, though I begin to sense the limitations of a film-making style which reveals an almost solipsistic lack of interest in character. His films are "about" situations, never about people. They resemble the novels of Anthony Burgess who – so S.K. says – "suddenly" began to denounce A Clockwork Orange after having praised it keenly for a long time. Burgess too confuses innovation with originality. By never doing the same thing twice, yet never reaching a new level of achievement, he displays a kind of monotonous versatility. Like Kubrick, he is a Proteus who ceaselessly, obsessively avoids being himself. The supreme paranoid personality fears others as a screen for his dread of the last enemy, his own mortality.

'I still have to believe in Kubrick's genius (whatever it may mean to assign people to that category). Imagine if all these too obsequious months have *not* been in the service of a transcendent talent! Yet I am more conscious all the time that he has constructed his infallibility around a wilful inability to consider any ideas which might require him to re-evaluate his own. Dependent on skills which he both envies and resents, he is in the usual state of directors who cannot write. His failure to dump me after the William Morris office fuck-up was, I suppose, the greatest compliment he is likely to pay me.

'I do not know him much better than I did at Christmas, though at much greater length. Perhaps he is an enigma without a secret, a man who has abandoned motives: there is no sense in trying to divine the psychological make-up of someone who is no longer interested in himself. He limits self-knowledge to having inflexible ambitions. I have to hope that making this film is still one of them. Can he really consider *Eyes Wide Shut* a "poetic" title? Perhaps its charm is that it is undoubtedly of his own composition. If it incites him to make the movie, so be it. Let's hope that he has not reached the state which reduced Jack Clayton to total, if fastidious, impotence. It is seven years since *Full Metal Jacket*, a title of which he seems unduly proud, if only because it is so cryptic (in the same spirit, Nabokov was rather childishly proud of composing unfathomable anagrams). *Full Metal Jacket II* would not be a bad title for S.K. After all this time, he still wears an impermeable carapace. I do not know whether (let alone how much) he likes me or my work. He can make very civil efforts to be amiable.

'He never explains why he doesn't like a scene, especially when he has to concede that it is pretty funny. I have come to see that he distrusts my jokes – any jokes – probably because a well-scripted passage of dialogue which presages a climactic laugh demands that the scene be shot precisely to that end. Joe (*All About Eve*) Mankiewicz used to say that a good script had, in some sense, been directed already. That is not the kind of script Kubrick will ever want. Anything too *finished* leaves him with an obligation to obedience. The only kind of rebel he is, in fact, is a rebel against being told what to do. No one could be less like Stanley Donen, who defined his own achievement by his success in honouring the talents of others. He is like a great conductor who does not need regularly to convince himself that he also composed the music.

'Kubrick is a creator who may recruit the best acolytes he can find, but who can never grant them freedom, least of all a licence to improve *him* or to share his loneliness. There are no trinities in his theology. He can be jested with, but he cannot be questioned (the whores who were hired to service the Emperor Louis-Napoleon were told, "You may kiss His Majesty anywhere except on his *face*"). That self-protective tangle of beard, the barbed wiriness of it, keeps other people's faces away from his own. He hides in an anonymous thicket. He may not always have been so reclusive, but his agoraphobia is now so pronounced that it is stronger than he is. Perhaps he struggles against it, but in vain. I sent him a card, and a catalogue, for Sarah's show at Agnew's. He called the day *after* it took place and said he was unable to come. My daughter's pictures looked pretty interesting though. He even took the trouble to listen to her interview on *Woman's Hour* and told me what a beautiful voice she had. Nice.

'He asked me about my experiences with hookers or at orgies. On both topics I had to disappoint him. However, what concerns him is always the furniture, the mechanics of such things, never what anyone might *feel* (how do you photograph sentiments?). He mocked my desire that the script should have a shape – which it will now have – but form (and its deformation, as in *Full Metal Jacket*) is his only defence against chaos and indecision. He has convinced himself that our salvation lies in keeping to Schnitzler's "beats"; if anything goes wrong, deviation from "Arthur" has to be the reason for it. At the outset, he gave the impression that all kinds of elements might be added (including Bill and Alice splitting up), but now that the graft with New York has taken, he wants as straight a translation as can be. Please God he doesn't go back on having the climactic scene I have lobbied for between Bill and Ziegler. Sometimes (i.e. very often), I feel that I have been asked for a lift by a man who claims to admire both my driving and the power of my vehicle and who then, as I accelerate, asks why I have released the hand-brake.'

S.K.: Freddie? Stanley. Can you talk?

F.R.: Of course.

S.K.: Are you OK?

F.R.: What's the problem, Stanley?

S.K.: OK, so . . . I got the pages. That's a pretty funny last scene you've written between Bill and Ziegler.

F.R.: It's not meant to be *just* funny. Do you think it works?

S.K.: If I could get the right actors, that's a great scene.

F.R.: Who are you thinking of?

S.K.: Bogart and Greenstreet. If I could get them, I'd say that was just the scene we needed. But I can't. So . . . would you think about it again?

F.R.: I can't believe it's impossible to find actors who could do the scene. A good scene doesn't really depend just on specific actors, does it?

S.K.: It has that kind of rhythm, you know, that ... says Bogart and Greenstreet. I don't think we have actors who could do it the way you wrote it.

F.R.: You want me to make it ... *duller*? It can't just be an explanation, can it? It needs to be about something else at the same time.

S.K.: I don't know.

F.R.: It ought to be *dramatic*, don't you think so?

S.K.: Dramatic? How?

F.R.: Stanley, don't worry, I'll do it again, OK? That's not the problem. But, as I see it, it can't just be that Ziegler tells Bill that he's taken care of everything and that there will be no consequences because he owed him one...

S.K.: What's your point?

F.R.: OK. To put it bluntly, I see it as a kind of a love scene. I'm not saying things shouldn't be ... cleared up, plot-wise, but it can be a love scene as well. In the sense that there's a kind of Oedipal thing going on between Ziegler and Bill. Ziegler is the demanding, protective, castrating father.

S.K.: Would you do it again?

I did it again, and again. The fourth or fifth version was, of course, blanched of nearly all the duplicity which had made it alive for me. I was back compiling a colour-it-yourself book to which Stanley would add his own characteristic tones. He wanted the spaces to have seductive outlines, but not to carry any instructions. He was not about to direct by numbers. Other directors may ask, 'How do we do it, how do we do it?' Not Stanley; if he didn't know how to do it, it would not be done; it would not be him.

When Henry James finally accepted that he could never rival Oscar Wilde (the triumphant first night of *The Importance of Being Earnest* coincided with the catastrophic opening of James's *Guy Domville*), he looked back ruefully on his theatrical failure. A friend asked him whether he could explain why his plays were flops. Were they too intellectual? James doubted it. 'After all,' he said, 'I tried so hard to be base.'

For anyone who writes for performance rather than print, baseness need involve no more than the concession to others of the final word. The more often a scene is rewritten, the more you are disposed to give them (*whoever they are!*) what they want. My euphoria when I was first approached by Kubrick was due, in no small part, to the assumption that he would accept only my best work and that he would come clean about his vision of the movie. Towards the end of more than seven months, I recognized that so far he had been only his own producer; the script had not yet docked, so to speak, with his directorial intelligence. His genius showed itself only in his infinite capacity to keep me plugging away. From time to time, he would supply me with a computerized grid, setting out the timetable, as it were, for the next term of effort on my part. If I was inventively deviant, the bell rang and brought me back to the party line. Having agreed to my idea for the ending, he still asked me, politely, to 'follow the boxed A.S. outline'.

By mid-June, it seemed that I might have some part of the summer free of bondage. The script had been worked and worked again, and again. I dreamed of running into the stadium after my second successive marathon and of *almost* having withdrawal symptoms if I was not asked to try a third time. Stanley's faxes approached enthusiasm: 'Thank you for the pages which are [*sic*] fine except for the dream which seems a bit wordy. Say it out loud at acting speed...'

It was good advice; I wish that executives would follow it more often. They will read a scene without listening to its undertones. John Malkovitch once complained to me that in a given scene his character was saying what he genuinely felt. He found it impossible to act unless the words he uttered were, in some way, at odds with what the character really meant or felt. If Kubrick's plan was never consciously to give uncontrollable opportunities to actors, still less to depend on them to supply extra meaning to a scene, he was alert to the danger of cramming their mouths with words. Had he learnt the lesson from his only truly disappointing movie, *Lolita*? To my mind, he deferred too unconditionally to Nabokov's brilliant word-play. Neither James Mason's mellifluous Humbert Humbert nor Peter Sellers' clowning riffs as Clare Quilty could make a film out of verbosity. Stanley told me that Mason's apparent effortlessness was the result of intense, and anguished, effort. During the making of *Lolita*, he had the habit of clenching his hands so tightly that, at the end of the days, the nails had drawn blood from the palms. He wore the stigmata of his genius. To my knowledge, no female star excited Kubrick's admiration as Sellers or Mason or Rossiter did. Stanley's sacred cows were all masculine. He said to me one day, 'Did you ever see *Gone with the Wind*?'

'Yes, I have. Hasn't everybody?'

'Did you ever see a worse performance than Vivien Leigh in *Gone with the Wind*? Has to be one of the worst performances ever. You know something? It's really a terrible movie.'

Kubrick might have wanted me to tell him everything I could imagine, when I first set about naturalizing Albertina and Fridolin in New York, but he grew increasingly impatient with the verbiage he had solicited. It is said that Giacometti sometimes tried to break with habit and make fatter sculptures. He always reduced them (sometimes at the very last moment) to anorexic proportions. Kubrick now wanted a script without novelistic fat. His curiosity was quickly satisfied if what you told him, or did for him, did not appeal to his peculiar appetites.

If I longed for release, it was a matter of professional honour not to show it. Somewhat like Malkovitch, I took consolatory pleasure in saying what I did not mean, not least that I was perfectly willing to do a scene again. It was not until the end of June that I sent off the last batch of pages for the last time. I added a more chatty covering fax than usual. I ended by saying, 'Do you know the story about the man who was having a pair of trousers made by a Jewish tailor and it was taking forever? Two months, three months, *six* months. Finally he said to the tailor, "It took the good Lord six *days* to make the world and you it takes six months to make a pair of pants?" And the tailor said, "So look at the world, and then just look at this pair of pants." Why does this story occur to me at this stage? Best regards, Freddie.'

S.K.: Freddie? How are you?

F.R.: I'm OK.

S.K.: I think it's turned into a pretty good scene.

F.R.: Yeah? I'm still sorry you couldn't get Bogart and Greenstreet.

S.K.: Seems we're pretty well there. I get the feeling you're kinda close to done on this, aren't you?

F.R.: If you're sure you're happy.

S.K.: I'll tell Warners to pay you whatever they owe you. Are you going to Wimbledon?

F.R.: We're going to France. What're you going to do this summer?

S.K.: I guess I better try and get this picture made.

F.R.: Great. How will you do that?

S.K.: Go over it until I think it's ... pretty well in shape. And then what I'll do is, I'll call Terry Semel and ask him to get over here.

F.R.: Then what happens?

S.K.: What happens is, he flies over and I put him in a hotel in London and I don't call him for about twenty-four hours. So he gets good and rested and a little bit ...

F.R.: Nervous?

S.K.: Eager. Let's say eager. And then what I do is, I send a car and bring him out to the house and I sit him down in a room and I give him the script to read and I tell him this is the picture I want to make. What's he going to do? He's come all the way to England, he's sitting in my house, what can he do?

F.R.: If you need me, you know where to find me.

'He guesses he'd better try and get the picture made. First time he's said anything about making it.'

Sylvia said, 'I hope it's been worth it.'

'Please God my epitaph won't be just "He worked with Stanley Kubrick. Once."'

'And please God it doesn't say *twice*.'

'He's the best.'

'He'd better be.'

'What do you say we go out to dinner? Time to celebrate. Even if I'm not exactly sure what.'

'Survival?'

School was out. I almost missed it. Without the goad of Stanley's almost daily demands, Sisyphus hardly knew where to roll his stone. When the telephone rang, and it was *not* the long dreaded Stanley, I was something like disappointed. My burden had been a privilege; the freed slave missed his chains. I missed spending hours and hours in the private space of conversations with a man to whom few other people ever had access. There was never any doubt who was the courtier and who the sovereign, but had not even Voltaire relished something of the same unequal intimacy with Frederick the Great?

I turned with relieved autonomy to the novel on which I had had to postpone work. One day, I had a handwritten fax from Stanley telling me that his time had been badly chopped up by the demands of preparation but that 'all goes well'. He hoped the same for me. When I came to scripting *The Thought Gang*, it was as if some department of my mind had gone over to him: despite myself, I kept wondering whether he would like what I was doing.

As weeks and then months went by, all without a single word from him, I began to think that all those hundreds and hundreds of pages had been written in vain. Perhaps he had decided to switch to something quite different: New York under water perhaps.

In the early autumn I heard on the William Morris grapevine that Tom Cruise and Nicole Kidman had 'passed' on it. Would Stanley look elsewhere or would the whole thing go away?

I elected to be literally philosophical: with Ray Monk, the biographer of Wittgenstein and of Bertrand Russell, I undertook to edit a series of monographs about great philosophers. A nucleus of very able academics and writers rallied to our call and I was soon playing the common reader to their expert texts.

One day in mid-December, I received a fax from Stanley telling me that he had completed his work on the script and made a deal with Warners and cast Tom Cruise and Nicole Kidman. He added that although a couple of people at W.B. had been told the author and title of the book, it would still not be publicly identified. He would appreciate it if I and 'the trusted Ron would continue to faithfully observe this stricture'. He then asked if I would be able to 'come out to the house one day during the holidays', have lunch and then sit in a room with tea and biscuits for an hour or so and read what he had been doing. 'Best regards, Stanley.'

His note seemed more shy than abrupt. He broke his good news like a child confessing, all but sulkily, that he had come top of the class. I wondered what kind of work he had done on the script and, almost dispassionately, what kind of a job he had made of it. Cruise and Kidman! Wow!

I found a Folio Society edition of Suetonius's *Lives of the Caesars* (in which Julius did not, of course, figure) and wrapped it for him. Once again a St Albans cab came to call for me at noon. Once again we took the devious road to the Kubrick estate.

INT/EXT. THE CAB. HERTFORDSHIRE. DAY.

F.R. – in corduroy trousers, leather jacket, open-necked shirt – sits in the back of the cab. Can we tell from his posture or the slight smile on his lips just how he feels about his fourth visit

to the Kubrick house? Does he expect trouble or disappointment? Is he wise not to have eaten before leaving
London?

He looks out of the window as the cab turns in through the
elaborate gates and what was once surprising is now familiar
décor. There is something more comic than impressive about
the warning signs, the sleeping policemen, the gates at which
the DRIVER is required to descend and press buttons.

Here we are again! Familiarity breeds less contempt than a
kind of unsurprised amazement that KUBRICK should live
here of all possible places and in such an atmosphere of
pampered apprehension. How grand yet how unpretentious
it still is! F.R. thinks of the space station which Bill Sylvester
visits in *2001*.

EXT. THE KUBRICK HOUSE. DAY.

F.R. steps out on to the gravel and walks towards the front
door with his briefcase as the cab circles and goes.

F.R. knocks on the door. A few seconds later STANLEY opens
it. He is wearing the usual denim outfit and his beard is still
untrimmed. He holds out a small white hand.

                    STANLEY
              Hi, Freddie. You OK?

                     F.R.
              How are you, Stanley?

                    STANLEY
              We can go through here, OK?

He leads the way through the house which seems even more than before to be a huge repository. The Christmas season has put pressure on the staff who remain so unobtrusive that it is as if F.R. is alone with STANLEY, even though he can hear sounds of activity.

> STANLEY
> You been working?

> F.R.
> And some. You too, right?

INT. THE BILLIARD ROOM. KUBRICK HOUSE. DAY.

There are no newspapers on the floor and that could be a new stack of electronic equipment, some of it still boxed, on the bare floor under the empty cue-racks.

On the long black refectory table is a plate of sandwiches and also a set of pages bound together by a black plastic spiral and with a transparent plastic cover through which can be seen a script with no title page.

> STANLEY
> Chicken OK with you?

> F.R.
> Chicken's fine.

> STANLEY
> You want some coffee?

> F.R.
> Have you eaten?

STANLEY

I'm OK.

F.R.

Coffee would be nice. So you cast the
picture.

STANLEY

Are you willing to read what I did to
the script?

F.R.

Isn't that why I'm here? Have they read
it? Cruise and Kidman?

STANLEY

They came out here to the house. By
helicopter.

F.R.

You don't say.

STANLEY

Sure they did. Landed right out there
on the lawn.

F.R.

Very unassuming.

STANLEY

Sat right over there while I told them
about the picture. They held hands. It
was sweet. Now and again they'd kinda
consult together. He'd look at her,
she'd look at him and he'd say, 'OK,
Nic?' and she'd say, 'If it is with you.'

They're a truly married couple. It was
kinda touching. She's agreed to give
me a couple of days when she takes off
her clothes. I guess we'll close the set.
Might be a good day to happen to drop
by the studio, if you wanted to.

F.R.
Very tempting, but I bet I don't do it.
I'm kinda ... silly, but it's like taking
advantage, you know what I mean? I
had it happen another time with
something of mine ... very good-
looking woman, but ...

He remembers when they were shooting *The Glittering Prizes*
and Barbara Kellerman said, 'Do you want pubes and everything?' He could easily have stayed to watch, but he didn't.

STANLEY
So anyway ... on the script ...

F.R. arranges a certain wilful amusement on his face. He senses
that KUBRICK is a little nervous and politely does nothing
to make things easier for him. Why should he?

STANLEY
This is ... what I did in the summer,
OK?

F.R.
Fine.

STANLEY

Will you look at it and tell me what
you really think?

F.R.

I shall be happy to.

STANLEY

Best if I leave you alone to do that.

F.R.

Probably.

STANLEY

So that's what I'll do. Here are some
numbers to call me when ... you've
finished. If ... you have some things
you want to say. Will you be OK?

F.R.

I shall be fine.

STANLEY

You'll probably find some things that're
... kinda ... rough.

F.R.

That's OK.

STANLEY

So, those are the numbers, when you're
ready, to call. Coffee. I'll ... have that
taken care of.

F.R. smiles tenderly at STANLEY. Perhaps for the first time
he can imagine that he knows exactly how the great

director feels. There is something touching in his gruff nervousness.

STANLEY

(At the door)

Take all the time you need.

F.R. nods. The door closes behind KUBRICK. F.R. pulls the plastic folder towards him. It is not very thick: less than a hundred pages. He sees that it is not written in film script form at all. Schnitzler's story has been rendered once again as a prose narrative. F.R. smiles, slightly, ruefully (?), at the Giacometti effect: the hundreds of pages he has supplied have been reduced, like a great chef's sauce, to dense skimpiness.

A blonde GIRL comes in with a pot of coffee, milk and sugar. F.R. thanks her with an air of amusement, as if she must be aware of the comedy of the situation in which he has been invited to sit in judgement on KUBRICK. She shows no sign of complicity.

F.R. reads quickly, as one might a review, urgent for good news and afraid of bad. How much of his dialogue remains? Are there manifest signs of genius in the collapsed text? F.R. pushes down the plunger in the coffee pot and tells himself to eat a thick sandwich.

He smiles. He sighs. He moves his chair slightly. Is he displeased by what he reads? He is relieved not to be impressed, or greatly affronted. He recognizes skeins of his own dialogue and finds little to admire in the places where KUBRICK has cut or simplified it. He finds little to alarm him, and not much to admire. The eighty-five or so pages are a blueprint for a movie. They contain only enough words to remind the director of what he means to do or have people say.

F.R. reads with his pen in his hand. From time to time, he makes exclamatory marks in the margin. Now and again, he winces and writes in a comment: 'Must we? Really? *Really*?', etc.

F.R. finishes his first reading in half an hour, incuding time to chew the sandwiches and drink the thin coffee. He looks out of the window at the already darkening winter afternoon.

> NARRATOR
>
> Is he thinking of his months of effort
> to please and astonish? How much of
> that dedication was worth the trouble?
> Kubrick has retained some of F.R.'s
> ideas and lines, but as often he has
> replaced them with banality. F.R. is
> neither pleased nor displeased. Kubrick
> has swallowed all the drafts, digested
> and regurgitated them.

F.R. looks at the telephone and at the numbers which STANLEY has left for him to call. He pushes the numbers away and takes a deep breath. He imagines KUBRICK somewhere in the great house. Is he dreading F.R.'s call? Is he making out that he is too busy and too brilliant to be concerned with F.R.'s opinions?

> NARRATOR
>
> F.R. does not often talk to himself. He
> makes few plans and practises little
> self-control. But now he tells himself,
> consciously and wilfully, to think
> before he calls Kubrick. Why has he
> been called? What does Kubrick want

of him? And what does he want of
Kubrick? The text is jejune and
without literary grace. It is almost
gauche in its unpretentiousness.
Occasionally it is embarrassing. F.R.
takes no pleasure in this opinion, nor
does he mean to conceal his criticism.
He is, for this afternoon at least,
Kubrick's judge. He has the producer's
part and the producer has his. It is a
brief Saturnalia, when the master is the
slave and vice versa. There is no hurry
to relieve Stanley of his anxiety.

F.R. pulls the folder towards him and again takes out his pen.
He sets himself to re-read the text and this time he does not
hesitate to defile it with exclamation marks, question marks
and words of one clear syllable. Having decided to find whatever faults he can, he abandons tact for honesty. Why else is
he here? KUBRICK must know that there is still work to do.
Does he want F.R. to do it or not? F.R. has the small pleasure
of seeing that he can put the master in check.

As F.R. deliberately chews his way through the last sandwich
and drains the tepid coffee, he remembers part of one of those
long conversations on the telephone:

F.R.: I was talking to a man who says he remembers you
playing chess in New York City.

S.K.: Yeah?

F.R.: He told me he saw you playing this four- or five-year-old
girl in some outdoor place in the Village.

S.K.: I don't think so.

F.R.: He swears it was you and she'd been coached in the first dozen or so moves of some fancy opening and she had you in trouble.

S.K.: I don't remember playing outside in New York City.

F.R.: Do you still play?

S.K.: I quit. I have a computer or two I look at sometimes, but ... I don't play with ... you know ... other people.

F.R.: But you used to, right?

S.K.: Sure. I played chess pretty seriously at one point.

F.R.: What was the most serious?

S.K.: Depends what you mean by serious. I played with some Arab prince one time. That was pretty serious. He had this ivory-handled pistol in his belt. He heard I played chess so he challenged me to a game.

F.R.: What happened? Did you accept?

S.K.: It was his house, there were a lot of people around, it was kinda hard not to. Yes, I did. He said he was pretty good. He had this fancy chess set in the next room he took me into.

F.R.: Good players don't like to play with fancy pieces too much, do they?

S.K.: Probably not. But he had this fancy set he liked to play with. He closed the door and we played a game. He wasn't bad, he wasn't good.

F.R.: You won?

S.K.: I won pretty quickly.

F.R.: So what happened?

S.K.: He wanted to play again. What could I do? We played again. I figured he didn't want to go back in the other room too fast.

F.R.: And what happened the second time?

S.K.: I made a mistake...

F.R.: And let him win?

S.K.: And didn't.

F.R.: You won again! Was that wise?

S.K.: Probably not. But ... that's what happened.

F.R.: What did he do?

S.K.: He didn't pull his gun exactly, but ... He showed it to me. He ... made me aware of it. And then he smiled, not too much of a smile, and he said we should go back in the other room where everyone was. He patted me on the shoulder and let me go through first. I didn't feel too ... easy about his attitude, but he was OK. When they asked him who'd won, he looked at me and then he said, 'We each drew a game.' I didn't argue. Anyone who knew anything about chess would know it was ridiculous. And anyone who didn't, so what?

F.R.: Do you know the story about Greg Peck and Willie Wyler?

S.K.: I don't think so.

F.R.: Peck was producing and starring.

S.K.: OK.

F.R.: And the first day, Peck suggested Willie shoot a close-up of him. Stanley Donen told me this story. Willie said he didn't need a close-up and Greg said it would be a good idea to shoot it in case. Willie said they'd pick it up when they had time. He kept putting it off and finally Greg, as producer, threatened to close the picture down if Willie didn't do this particular close-up. The studio people came down and begged him not to endanger the whole picture, so Willie said OK, he'd do it before the end of the shoot. Greg said, 'Do I have your word? Because otherwise I'm walking right off this set.' And Willie said, 'You have my word.' They went right through the last day of shooting and they still hadn't done this particular close-up. They did the last set-up and Willie said that it was a wrap. End of shooting. Greg couldn't believe that he still hadn't had his close-up. Willie said it was too late. Greg said, 'You promised. You gave me your word. How can you do this?' Willie said, 'Know something, Greg? A man holds a pistol to my head, there isn't anything I won't promise.'

S.K.: That's right. So listen, I'll talk to you tomorrow, OK?

F.R. has pulled the telephone towards him and presses the numbers which STANLEY has written on the piece of paper.

F.R.

(Into phone)
OK, so I read that.

F.R. imagines STANLEY walking through the house towards the billiard room. What does he hope to hear? What does diplomacy and/or self-interest dictate that he should hear?

F.R. opens the pages to a place where there is no shortage of scribbles in the margin and on the widely spaced print.

STANLEY comes in. Can he be seen as the bearded pupil coming to see his tutor? Why not

> F.R.
>
> It seems fine. On the whole. What shall
> we do? Do you want to go through it
> or what? Because . . .

F.R.'s voice is, he likes to suppose, tender and implacable.

STANLEY sits down next to him.

> F.R.
>
> I don't know what you wanted me to
> do exactly, but I've made quite a lot of
> marks. There are things that . . . I really
> don't think I'd do.

> STANLEY
>
> Listen, I'm not a writer. I know that.

I had my moment of domination, but I did not – could not – prolong it. I had no illusion that I had a pistol in my belt, still less that I could hold it to Stanley's head. I went through the script page by page and, without posturing or foolishness, I pointed out where there were weaknesses or lines that would not play well. I reminded him that he had once advised me, quite rightly, to speak the dialogue aloud and weigh it on the tongue. He listened attentively and, so far as I could judge, without resentment. The longer we talked, the more there seemed to be in the text that needed attention. By the end, I was reassuring Stanley that the line was clear and sharp and that I had no quarrel with the overall shape. I had, after all, argued at great length for the dénouement which I was pleased to see that he had not changed substantially, although Bogart and Greenstreet were not available. He seemed relieved. He asked, almost humbly, whether I was willing to go through it one more time for him.

'Of course I am,' I said. 'Do you want to keep this narrative form?'

'It's more real to me when it doesn't read like one more script. That's why...'

'I'll do it the same way. Keep it short this time, right?'

'Think you can?'

'I think so.'

'When can you start?'

'Right after Christmas. If I don't keep sending you pages, I should be able to do it faster than...'

'OK. You're due another payment. I'll fix for that to happen right away.'

He seemed relieved and even grateful. I was not grateful, but I was relieved: he had indeed digested my work, but its shape and much of its detail were there in his rescript. I understood very well, and without rancour, that he had had to possess the script (as cannibals do the force of their respected adversaries) by swallowing it. It may be amusing and often truthful to portray directors as presumptuous predators, but Kubrick had to convince himself that what he would film was compatible with his creative persona; it had, so to say, to pass through his gut.

I left him *The Lives of the Caesars* and was handed a very thick, neatly wrapped package for myself. It seemed more like Christmas as I left than it had as I knocked on the door. Stanley came out on to the forecourt as my taxi came through the last of the electric barriers.

'So listen,' he said, 'thanks for ... coming out. And for everything you did.'

'And will do,' I said.

'Worked out pretty well, didn't it?' He put his arm around my shoulder. I was aware of the small white hand gleaming in the light from the front door. Showbiz is full of insincere bear-hugs; a lot of them leave teethmarks. Kubrick had never been effusive. It was the first time he had done more than shake hands in a hurry. I recalled the look that Peter Sellers, as Group-Captain Lionel Mandrake, had given to Jack D. Ripper's hand as it squeezed his shoulder. I felt more affection than apprehension. There was a wary warmth in Stanley's embrace which made it more unguarded, and flattering, than anything he ever said to me.

I said, 'I wouldn't have missed it, Stanley.'

I got into the taxi and was driven towards the first gate. Then I realized that I didn't have his text with me. I got out and ran back to the house and rang the bell. He opened the door.

'I forgot the script.'

'I have it for you.'

'We could analyse that, if we wanted to,' I said. 'But we don't, do we?'

'I don't think so.'

He smiled and I went back to the cab and got in. I waved to him through the window as if, although I should never trade on it, we were now closer friends. I never saw him again.

Despite having already done countless rewrites, I attacked what Stanley had done with some zeal. It was a neat opportunity to be aggressively useful. What he had written had laid him open to scorn, or at least condescension, and he was, I think, relieved when I preferred to be constructive. I was pleased, above all, by the certainty that the picture was going to be made. Cruise and Kidman promised that it would be seen everywhere, but Stanley had not cast them only because they were box office. His admiration for Cruise was based in particular on his performance in *Born on the Fourth of July*. Tom had Stanley's ambitious dedication: for both of them, there was no choice between doing things as well as you could and any other possibility.

The care with which I revised and amplified the script exceeded the 'polish' stipulated in my contract. It was a liberation to go beyond the line of duty. While I was working, I sent Stanley a copy of the script of *The Thought Gang*, which I had completed during the previous summer.

S.K.: Freddie? Can you talk?

F.R.: Hello, Stanley. How goes it?

S.K.: I've got a shit-load of work to do, I can tell you that.

F.R.: When are you planning to shoot?

S.K.: How's it coming?

F.R.: Pretty good. I'll send you a big chunk in a week or two.

S.K.: Because, you know, there's a lot we have to do.

F.R.: I know.

S.K.: I read the script you did for your son.

F.R.: Yes?

S.K.: Pretty damn good dialogue.

F.R.: Yeah, well . . .

S.K.: I think you're going to make a shit-load of money out of it. I'd green-light it right away if it was my decision.

F.R.: That's pretty good to hear.

S.K.: What's the name of that French actor? Dooper-doo?

F.R.: Dooper-doo? Dépardieu!

S.K.: Gerard, right? How would you pronounce that?

F.R.: (*Très à la française*) Gérard Dépardieu.

S.K.: (After a pause) OK. So, how would I pronounce it?

F.R.: I think you'd probably say Gerard Depardoo.

S.K.: That's who you should get. And maybe Tony Hopkins.

F.R.: And Miou-Miou, I thought. You know her?

S.K.: I'd give it a green light right away. Tell your son that.

F.R.: He'll be very pleased, and grateful. So'm I.

S.K.: If you want me to say something to people, I will, tell him.

F.R.: That's really nice of you.

S.K.: So when do you think I can have a bunch of pages?

Reading other people's scripts is rarely a pleasure. Stanley's promptness and encouragement were very generous. As it turned out, Paul and I did not have occasion to take him up on his offer to put in a good word for us. Through an inadvertent failure to renew our option on Tibor Fischer's novel, and his refusal to allow us to repair it, we lost the underlying rights without which the script was valueless. Tibor was, of course, within his rights, but he was interdicted, by the copyright laws, from using any of my script (which he had vigorously endorsed). Perhaps he imagined that it would be easy to procure another screenplay based on his picaresque novel. Perhaps it will be.

I sent Stanley a fat chunk of thoroughly revised script and he asked only for minor changes to it. I suspect that his interest was now concentrated as much on the logistics of production and on the sweet burden of casting and designing his movie as on the text. After nine lean years, he was back in business as a director. The project was no longer something which passed back and forth between the two of us. He spoke to me with much less anxiety. Our long, secret and now, it seemed, successful struggle to make a viable movie out of Schnitzler turned us into buddies of a kind. We were veterans of the bonding process, with which Peter Pieter's Ed had threatened me in Paris.

It took several months of work before Stanley called me, in early June 1996, after I sent him the revised revisions to the last section of the script. We had been speaking regularly, and easily, but now he seemed shy once again.

S.K.: You really can do this stuff, can't you?

F.R.: Are you sure that last scene's what you want?

S.K.: It's close. I get the feeling you're pretty well done here, aren't you?

F.R.: I'll do it again, if you want me to.

S.K.: I told them to make the last payment, OK?

F.R.: That's not the point. If you don't like the scene, I'll do it again.

S.K.: Would you do that?

F.R.: Stanley, let's get something clear: if you want me to do more work, I'll do it. It's a completely different thing writing a screenplay before you know if anyone's going to make it and ... the way things are now.

S.K.: Isn't it? It sure is.

F.R.: When are you planning to start?

S.K.: Maybe August.

F.R.: Jesus!

S.K.: That's right.

F.R.: So listen, you know where I am. You want me for anything on the script, any time, call me.

S.K.: I have to go through the thing again, but I'll show it to you soon.

F.R.: I want you to make a great movie, that's the thing.

S.K.: There's a shit-load of work to do first, I'll tell you.

F.R.: I'm not sorry for you.

S.K.: No. It's not a bad life being a movie director, after all, is it?

F.R.: I would say not.

S.K.: Not that bad being a screenwriter, is it?

Eyes Wide Shut finally started shooting in November 1996, two years after I started work on the first draft of the script. Stanley had been trying to find a way to transfer Schnitzler's story to the screen for about a quarter of a century. I was kept regularly informed of what was going on, unofficially, but Stanley himself never called me again. Despite what he had said (when he told me that I was such a good director I was not coming on his set), I do not believe that I should have been unwelcome. However, I have always been shy of turning up where I have nothing specific to do.

Thanks in no small part to Kubrick, I began to receive many more urgent calls from California from producers who told me, as the Earl of Derby had Sir Richard Burton, that they had thought of me at once. My greatest pleasure, as I look back on the long and arduous experience of working on *Eyes Wide Shut*, is that I did something to enable Stanley Kubrick to make another movie.

I did not hear from him personally until last winter, when he had almost finished editing. He wrote asking me to come out to the house sometime soon so that he could show me what he had finally decided to shoot. I said that, as usual, I was ready when he was. I took time out to re-read the dialogue between Caesar and Vercingetorix.

At Christmas, he sent me a large volume of Lartigue's photographs. In it was a card which said, 'Dear Freddie, Looking forward to seeing you. Best Wishes, Stanley'.

In early March, I turned on the television in order to discover whether Newcastle had beaten Everton in the Cup. They had. A printed insert under the images of Newcastle's victory announced that Stanley Kubrick was dead. Immortals too can die.